Win
at
Wealth

Win
at
Wealth

A Practical Guide to Designing and Implementing your Financial Freedom Plan

SCOTT JOHNSON, CFP®, CPWA®

GRAMMAR
FACTORY
— EST° 2013 —

Published by Grammar Factory Publishing, an imprint of MacMillan Company Limited.

Grammar Factory Publishing
MacMillan Company Limited
25 Telegram Mews, 39th Floor, Suite 3906
Toronto, Ontario, Canada
M5V 3Z1

www.grammarfactory.com

Johnson, Scott.
Win at Wealth: A Practical Guide to Designing your Financial Freedom Plan / Scott Johnson.

Paperback ISBN 978-1-998756-70-4
Hardcover ISBN 978-1-998756-72-8
eBook ISBN 978-1-998756-71-1

1. BUS027030 BUSINESS & ECONOMICS / Finance / Wealth Management.
2. BUS050030 BUSINESS & ECONOMICS / Personal Finance / Money Management.
3. BUS050040 BUSINESS & ECONOMICS / Personal Finance / Retirement Planning.

Production Credits
Cover design by Designerbility
Interior layout design by Ashley Howell
Book production and editorial services by Grammar Factory Publishing

Grammar Factory's Carbon Neutral Publishing Commitment
Grammar Factory Publishing is proud to be neutralizing the carbon footprint of all printed copies of its authors' books printed by or ordered directly through Grammar Factory or its affiliated companies through the purchase of Gold Standard-Certified International Offsets.

Disclaimer
The material in this publication is of the nature of general comment only and does not represent professional advice. It is not intended to provide specific guidance for particular circumstances, and it should not be relied on as the basis for any decision to take action or not take action on any matter which it covers. Readers should obtain professional advice where appropriate, before making any such decision. To the maximum extent permitted by law, the author and publisher disclaim all responsibility and liability to any person, arising directly or indirectly from any person taking or not taking action based on the information in this publication.

This book is dedicated to my beloved wife, Marissa,
my loving daughter, Olivia, and the memory of my mom, Lucille.

Their unwavering support and love have been a source
of inspiration throughout this journey.

Disclosures

Past performance is not indicative of future results and diversification does not ensure a profit or protect against loss. All investments carry some level of risk, including loss of principal.

The examples used in the book are hypothetical and provided for illustrative purposes only. They are not intended to represent a specific investment product, and investors may not achieve similar results.

Fixed income is generally considered to be a more conservative investment than stocks, but bonds and other fixed income investments still carry a variety of risk such as interest rate risk, regulatory risk, reinvestment risk, credit risk, inflation risk, call risk, default risk, political risk, tax policy risk and liquidity risk in a rising interest rate environment.

There are material differences between direct investments in stocks and bonds and investment of insurance policy cash value. All investments carry risk, and insurance is subject to the claims-paying ability of the issuer. Different life insurance types carry different risks and may have different lapse considerations depending on the investment options, if any, with the policy. It is important to consider how different investments are taxed when withdrawn and how that can be different from life insurance cash value and death benefit, and how this may change over the life of the investment or policy. Some insurance policies have a flexible death benefit which may be affected by premium payments and cash values.

Neither the author or Baird provides tax or legal advice. It is strongly encouraged that readers speak with their tax or legal professional prior to acting on this information. The opinions expressed are those of the author and not necessarily those of Baird.

The information contained in this book is for informational and entertainment purposes and does not provide readers with enough information or advice that is sufficient to base an investment decision on. Further, the information presented in this book is from sources regarded as credible, but neither the author nor Baird has verified the accuracy or completeness of this material.

Neither the author nor Baird have any formal relationships or arrangements with any of the non-Baird resources listed or suggested above, and this should not be considered an endorsement of the products or services offered by these individuals or their firms.

ABOUT THE AUTHOR

Scott Johnson has over 28 years of experience in the wealth management industry. He has a Bachelor of Arts degree in Business/Economics from Wheaton College (IL) and is a CERTIFIED FINANCIAL PLANNER® professional and a Certified Private Wealth Advisor®.

Using his Win at Wealth process, he has helped hundreds of individuals and families make decisions with their money so that they are freed up to pursue what is most important to them.

Scott and his wife, Marissa, have been married since 2000 and have one daughter, Olivia.

***

Certified Financial Planner Board of Standards Center for Financial Planning, Inc. owns and licenses the certification marks CFP®, CERTIFIED FINANCIAL PLANNER®, and CFP® (with plaque design) in the United States to Certified Financial Planner Board of Standards, Inc., which authorizes individuals who successfully complete the organization's initial and ongoing certification requirements to use the certification marks.

Investment & Wealth Institute™ (The Institute) is the owner of the certification marks "CPWA" and "Certified Private Wealth Advisor." Use of CPWA and/or Certified Private Wealth Advisor signifies that the user has successfully completed The Institute's initial and ongoing credentialing requirements for investment management professionals.

CONTENTS

*Good planning and hard work lead to prosperity,
but hasty shortcuts lead to poverty.*

PROVERBS 21:5

*To accomplish great things, we must not only act,
but also dream; not only plan, but also believe.*

ANATOLE FRANCE

INTRODUCTION

A s Michael and Amy sat down with me to start our meeting, their anxiety practically filled the room. I could almost hear the question they were asking themselves in their heads: "Will we ever be able to achieve Financial Freedom?"

Michael and Amy were in their late forties, successful professionals who both had long tenures in their respective fields. They thought that they had already taken many of the proper steps to put themselves in a position to retire, such as contributing to their workplace retirement plans, limiting debt, and setting aside savings for emergencies. While doing all this they had also raised three children, and helped them get through college and get established in their own independent lives. Even still, as our meeting began, I could see that they were still filled with concerns about their financial future.

I started by asking them a series of questions to clarify exactly what Financial Freedom looked like to them. They described it as wanting to continue enjoying their current lifestyle centered on their hobbies, staying connected with their kids wherever they may live, and being able to take a big vacation each year. When I asked them about timelines, they said that they wanted to achieve these goals within the next five to seven years. But just by how they answered, I could tell that they thought that would be next to impossible.

I've seen this hundreds of times throughout my 28 years as a financial advisor. It is one of the biggest sources of anxiety when it comes to planning—simply not knowing where you are in relation to your goals. This uncertainty can then lead to inactivity, which makes your goals more difficult to achieve. The good news, though, is that with just a little bit of effort and some organization, you can determine your "goal gap"—the distance between where you are now and where you would like to end up. In fact, by the end of this book, you will have this information in hand so that you can begin making better progress on your most important goals.

This is exactly what happened for Michael and Amy. Throughout our conversation, I assured them that it was way too early to assume that their goal was already out of reach. We then kept talking so that I could find out exactly where they were with their wealth, and how much income they would need to fund their desired lifestyle. This is the gap that they needed to cross on their wealth journey, and was at the very core of their financial plan. For, once we have this information, we can then accurately determine the action steps that need to be taken. This is what we would discuss at our next meeting a couple of weeks out, when we would review their written plan.

As we said goodbye at that first meeting, Michael and Amy said that they felt a little better about things just by talking it out and knowing that they were finally beginning to really organize their plan. However, they were still clearly apprehensive of what lay ahead for them, and doubtful that they had the resources and ability to realize their goals.

But they would be in for a big surprise when we met again in a few weeks.

The Need for Planning

Michael and Amy are far from alone in their peer group in both their lack of retirement planning, and their corresponding uncertainty about their financial future. Charles Schwab's Modern Wealth Index study for 2018 offered some interesting, and unsettling, facts about Generation X's ability to reach its long-term financial goals.[1] According to the report:

- only 20% of this cohort have a written financial plan,

- only 25% have specific savings goals, and

- only 16% work with a financial advisor.

If you're reading this right now, you can probably relate to at least one of these findings, and you know where you're falling short. You may know you need to have a written financial plan, but still haven't gotten around to it; or, if you do have one, maybe it's gathering dust in a desk drawer because you haven't looked at it since you designed it a few years ago. Maybe you're frustrated because you feel you should be making more progress on your savings goals than you are, but don't know how to go about doing it. And perhaps, even if you've begun to realize that you may need some help to get your wealth doing what you want it to do, the idea of seeking out a qualified advisor still feels like a bridge too far.

The common thread here is that you're frustrated about your lack of progress, and doubt your ability to reach your goals when you want to. You feel like you're treading water, or peddling furiously on a stationary bike and not even getting the fitness benefits. And you may even be beating yourself up about it, asking, "Why can't I make this happen for myself and the people I care about?"

The answer is not that you lack the resources, the cash flow, the ability, or the desire. Rather, it's because *you don't have a plan you believe in strongly enough to take the sustained action required to achieve your goals.*

This is what's creating the gap between where you are now, and where you want to be. And if this is the situation you're in, then you've come to the right place—because by the end of this book, you're going to have the plan you're missing. A plan that you can believe in. A plan that could help you achieve your goal of Financial Freedom on your terms, and overcome the fear that so many of us have felt in regard to our finances.

And believe me, that's a fear I know all too well. I grew up in a very middle-class family in northern Illinois, and while my siblings and I always had what we needed, we didn't have many of the extras that a lot of the other kids we knew did. Although our parents did their best, money was always a stress point in our household. I felt this stress particularly in middle and high school, as my father was often in and out of work. As I grew into early adulthood, the uncertainty of whether there would be enough money to pay the bills each month was always lurking in my mind, and it created a sense of fear and anxiety around money that led me to make some wrong decisions about how I managed my wealth when I first started living on my own.

After those bad early experiences, I knew I needed to change my thoughts about money to achieve my financial goals and feel more secure in my future. So, I decided to learn as much as possible about how to grow and manage wealth, figuring that the more I knew about the subject, the quicker I could overcome my unhealthy mindset regarding money. This led me to earn an undergraduate degree in business and economics, and then enter into a career in wealth management, where I continued to further my knowledge by obtaining professional designations as a CERTIFIED FINANCIAL PLANNER® Professional and Certified Private Wealth Advisor.

Now, I want to share that knowledge with you through this book, so that you too can experience the relief—and the joy—that I've seen in my clients time and time again, as the financial planning journey I embark on with them takes them from a place of anxiety and frustration to one of confidence in their financial future. This kind of knowledge really *is* helpful. With a proper financial plan in place, you will no longer be flying blind, but will have a clear view of the path to your own unique vision of Financial Freedom. That's the goal of this book—to help you create a plan you feel confident in, so that you can take the necessary (and sustained) action to achieve your Financial Freedom goals in the most efficient way possible.

A Plan You Can Believe In

Note the two key words in that last sentence: "confident" and "sustained." Those two qualities are inextricable from each other when it comes to building wealth, because if you don't have confidence in your plan, you will be much less likely to take the sustained action required to get you across the finish line. If this book helped you design a plan without also giving you the mental and emotional tools you need to execute it, the paper (or screen) it's written on would be of little value to you.

That's why this book is not some magic pill that you take just once to "cure" your financial ailments, nor some cookie-cutter, one-size-fits-all "rulebook" for building wealth. Rather, it's a *living document* that will help you design a custom plan fit to you and your goals that you can return to and mark up as you make progress towards them. By reading through this book and completing the exercises I've prepared for you, you won't just be following a map—you'll discover and chart the terrain of your own unique wealth journey.

The book is divided into three sections. In the first section (Chapters 1 to 4), you will learn how to envision and articulate what Financial Freedom means to you, and how to assemble the essential elements of an effective wealth plan. You will then learn how to recruit your financial "Dream Team" of experts and advisors who will help you devise and begin executing your plan, and stick by you to track and show you ways to accelerate your progress. Finally, you will learn how to assess the current state of your wealth in relation to where you want to go, identifying the gaps and obstacles you will have to bridge to arrive at your destination.

The second section (Chapters 5 to 7) will show you how to design an investment strategy that fits your unique situation, giving you the best probability of success while minimizing stress by making sure you can stay on track no matter what the investment markets throw at you. You will also learn some of the timeless investment principles that others have used to create and sustain wealth, and why it's important to focus on *passive investment cash flow* when developing your Financial Freedom investment strategy.

In the last section (Chapters 8 to 11), you will learn how to sustain your progress on your journey to Financial Freedom by minimizing the tax drag on your portfolio returns, and how to protect your wealth against the most common risks that could delay your success. You will also learn how to inherit wealth wisely and create an estate (legacy) plan to ensure your family's financial security in the generations to come. Lastly, we'll walk through how to track your progress as you move through your plan stage by stage.

Figure 1: Wealth management formula designed for financial freedom

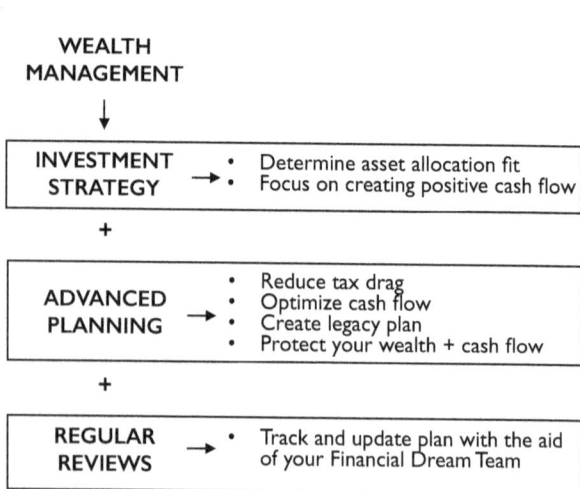

WEALTH MANAGEMENT

↓

| **INVESTMENT STRATEGY** → | • Determine asset allocation fit
• Focus on creating positive cash flow |

\+

| **ADVANCED PLANNING** → | • Reduce tax drag
• Optimize cash flow
• Create legacy plan
• Protect your wealth + cash flow |

\+

| **REGULAR REVIEWS** → | • Track and update plan with the aid of your Financial Dream Team |

The First Step

As you embark on your journey towards Financial Freedom, it's natural to feel apprehensive. Where you want to be can look so far away from where you are right now. You may be asking yourself: "What's the point of taking the first step in this marathon, if I know (or rather, feel) that there's no way I can make it to the finish line?"

I'll tell you why—because when you take that very first step, you can suddenly discover that you have the strength and stamina to take yourself the whole way. Just ask Michael and Amy.

When I sat down with Michael and Amy a second time, I told them about the pleasant surprise that was in store for them as we went through their plan. It turns out that they were much closer to achieving their goals than they thought—all they needed was some help organizing their financial life. Knowing this took them from a place of frustration and anxiety to one of confidence, and that confidence only grew as, over the next few years, they got to work earnestly on their plan, taking the necessary actions and making real progress on their goals. This diligence paid off, and I am happy to report that they are well on their way to reaching their goal within their targeted timeframe.

You, too, can achieve that goal of Financial Freedom, whatever it looks like to you—all you need to do is take that first step.

And at this point, that first step is easy: just turn the page.

PART 1

LAYING THE FOUNDATION FOR YOUR FINANCIAL FREEDOM GOALS

*The goal isn't more money. The
goal is living life on your terms.*
CHRIS BROGAN

*Working because you want to, not
because you have to, is financial freedom.*
TONY ROBBINS

CHAPTER 1

WHAT DOES FINANCIAL FREEDOM MEAN TO YOU?

Josh and Kelly had just received a sizable inheritance from Josh's parents' estate, and wanted to use it to help them achieve Financial Freedom by the time they were 60, which would be in about 10 years. They had started taking many of the beginning steps towards this goal, like paying down all debt other than their mortgage, maxing out their employer retirement plans, and building an emergency fund. However, even as they had done all this, they had never really figured out what Financial Freedom really meant to them—that is, what it was they actually *wanted* that freedom to be and to look like. They had a deadline, but not a destination.

Stop for a minute and imagine how it would feel to be able to pursue what is most inspiring and fulfilling to you without the stress of financial burdens. What a wonderful place to be! But you can't ever reach that place where *you* are fully in charge of the rest of your life without first clearly defining what that place *is*.

This is what we're going to be covering in this chapter: how to create a *vision* of what your own unique Financial Freedom will look and feel like, and, with that vision as your North Star, begin to accelerate your progress towards that goal.

The Power of a Vision

In September 1962, President John F. Kennedy made an audacious promise in a speech he delivered at Rice University in Texas: that the United States would send a man to the Moon within the decade.

"Why, some say, the Moon? Why choose this as our goal?" Kennedy asked rhetorically. "And they may well ask, why climb the highest mountain? Why, 35 years ago, fly the Atlantic? [...] We choose to go to the Moon in this decade and do the other things, not because they are easy, but because they are hard—because that goal will serve to organize and measure the best of our energies and skills. Because that challenge is one that we are willing to accept, one we are unwilling to postpone, and one which we intend to win, and the others, too."

At the time Kennedy spoke those words, it had been only a little more than a year since Alan Shepard had become the first American astronaut to travel into space, and seven months since John Glenn had completed an orbit of the Earth. But a mere seven years later, in the summer of 1969, 500 million people around the world witnessed through their television sets what was once only the stuff of fantasy: astronaut Neil Armstrong stepping out of a spacecraft, setting foot on the surface of the Moon, and uttering those legendary words, "That's one small step for man, one giant leap for mankind."

Now, unless you're a tech billionaire, conquering outer space is likely not your idea of Financial Freedom. But you may feel like achieving your ultimate financial goals while still being able to enjoy your life in the present is as impossible as landing a man on the Moon seemed for so many at the beginning of the 1960s. Maybe Kennedy himself didn't even think that a lunar landing was achievable within the decade when he delivered that speech in Texas, but the vision he presented was so compelling that it helped fuel public enthusiasm and support for a seemingly unreachable goal. And this is the same principle you can bring to your own financial journey: set your sights clearly on your outcome, and you will help generate the energy you need to make it a reality.

A Vision Creates Clarity

There's a Biblical proverb that says, "Where there is no vision, the people perish." Similarly, when it comes to Financial Freedom, if you don't have a vision of your ultimate goals, they, too, will perish. Or to put it another way, in the words of baseball legend and part-time philosopher Yogi Berra, "If you don't know where you're going, you'll end up somewhere else."

The bottom line is, without a vision, it's easy to lose sight of what we are trying to accomplish, and thus go off target and begin taking actions that don't align with our plan. The result is a much longer journey than we wanted to take, and one that could also come with extra costs and a higher degree of frustration.

Let's say that, like Josh and Kelly, you set yourself a goal of reaching Financial Freedom within the next 10 years, but don't have a vision of what that really means. Like them, you start doing some of the sensible things that you believe will help you make progress towards that still vague goal. But then, after a couple of years, you find yourself at a financial crossroads when the *now* suddenly seems to be more attractive than the *then*—perhaps a chance to upgrade to a new home, or to take that vacation you always dreamed of. Which path do you take?

Now, I'm definitely not suggesting that *not* seizing opportunities in the moment is always the best course of action; that we must *always* be looking to the future and putting off enjoyment in the present. But either way, having a clear vision of what your Financial Freedom is will allow you to make those kinds of choices with a greater understanding of the trade-offs involved, and how important those trade-offs are to you. And, for people who do have their eyes set on the future but don't yet know what their desired future looks like, it can help them focus their generally beneficial but also undirected savings and investment tactics in the present so that they can reach that goal.

The latter was certainly the case with Josh and Kelly. After they came to see me, we set about building a plan based on their own vision of Financial Freedom, which centered on traveling, enjoying their family more, and giving to charities near their hearts. With that vision locked in, they could not only develop an action plan to realize it, but also find the inspiration and sense of purpose to fuel those actions. Over time, Josh and Kelly gained ever greater confidence in their ability to reach their goal as they saw the strategy they had implemented getting them closer and closer to it.

So now, the question we need to start answering is: What does Financial Freedom really look like to *you*?

What Does Financial Freedom Mean to You?

A common definition of Financial Freedom is when you have enough savings and passive income to sustain your desired lifestyle without depending on a paycheck, employment, or a certain job or industry. For some, this can mean retirement—to be free of the need to ever work again. To others, it may mean the freedom to pursue a second career without regard to the income it provides, or the freedom to volunteer in their community more. Some may interpret it as the freedom to spend more time with their children and grandchildren, strengthening family bonds.

Simply put, Financial Freedom means different things to different people, but at its core it means allowing people to live on their own terms and pursue their own unique path to a truly fulfilling life without financial obligations, fears or hardships holding them back. So, the first thing you need to do as you chart your course towards Financial Freedom is reflect on what is really most important to you.

Let's start that process by answering a few key questions that are designed to help you define exactly what it is you're trying to achieve, and start forming a picture in your mind of how your life will be impacted once your vision is realized. The questions are broken out into four categories:

- your work;

- your attitude towards money;

- your relationships; and

- your interests.

As you work through the questions below, keep this other, larger question in the back of your mind: *What would my life look and feel like if I actually achieved what I'm writing out here?*

Above all, *don't rush* through your answers. The responses you provide below are a vital first step in both creating an effective plan, and sparking some of the energy and drive you need to see it through.

Work/Life

a) What would your ideal job be? Is it your current one?

b) What skills/degrees/knowledge do you need to acquire to pursue your ideal job?

c) What top professional goals would you still like to achieve?

d) What would you do with your time if you no longer had to work?

Money

a) What is the most important value that money provides to you?

b) What do you want your money to do for you? For others?

c) What is the most exciting thing that having additional money would allow you to do?

d) What are your three biggest fears or worries about money?

Relationships

a) Which are the most important relationships in your life?

b) What charitable organizations do you donate your time and/or treasure to?

c) What drives your commitment to these other people or organizations?

d) How would you like to use your wealth to support them?

Interests

a) What does your ideal week look like?

b) What would your ideal vacation look like?

c) What activities do you do in your free time that energize you?

d) Who or what would you spend more time with if you had greater flexibility?

Take a few minutes, or longer if needed, to write out your answers to these questions. They may seem simple and straightforward, but these are the fundamental building blocks of your Financial Freedom plan. They're your most important reasons of dreaming of that freedom in the first place.

Creating Your Vision Statement

Now that you've assembled the list of answers about what is most important to you in regard to your life and goals, the next step is to create a *vision statement* of how you will look, feel, and think once you have accomplished those goals. This statement can take whatever form works best for you: a written text, a vision board, a journal entry, etc. However you do it, though, the most important thing is that you make that vision as concrete and vivid for you as you can — because the more real it is for you, the more fuel it will give you to power through the obstacles on your path towards it.

So, how do you start creating your vision statement? Just follow the few steps below:

1. First, review your answers to the questions above. (If you haven't finished that step yet, go back and do so now.)

2. Then, complete the following statement based on your answers to these questions:

   Financial Freedom to me is the ability to _____ without being limited to the constraint of needing to work and without worrying about money.

3. Now, complete the statement below:

   I want to achieve my definition of Financial Freedom so that I can _____, _____ , and _____ .

4. Lastly, combine these two statements together in a simple structure like the one below:

   Financial Freedom means that I can _____ without being

limited by the constraint of needing to work, and without worrying about money so that I can pursue the following things that are the most important to me: _____, _____, and _____.

That's it—it's that simple! Remember, a vision doesn't have to be complicated to be compelling. The most important elements of a vision are those that are fundamental to what we value and cherish most in our lives. What better goals to work towards than those?

Leveraging Your Vision for Success

Congratulations! Now that you've written out your vision statement, you've taken the first step towards your goal of Financial Freedom.

So, what do you do now? How do you start leveraging that vision statement to start making real progress towards your goal?

The first step is easy: *Keep your vision statement with you, all the time.*

Write out your vision statement on two notecards: one that you can easily carry with you as you go about your day, and another one that you can keep on your nightstand. If it works better, you could also make it a screen saver on your phone. Then, commit to reading it first thing in the morning before you get out of bed, and again at night just before you go to sleep. Once you've made this a firm part of your daily routine, start reading it in free moments throughout your day.

Now, of course, your vision statement is not a magic spell—you're not going to conjure it into reality just by ritualistically reading the words. But, by committing to meditating on your statement every day, you will imprint it on your mind in a way that is deeper than simple memorization. Your statement will begin to program your brain to start devising ideas and actions that could help make that vision a reality.

And, as more and more of these ideas start flowing out, reading turns to writing. You can start jotting down these notions as they come to you, thus building a larger structure on top of the foundation of your vision statement. And the more detailed this structure gets, the more your goals will be front of mind when you are faced with the kind of crossroads we described above. It can serve as a "decision filter" that will help ensure you are staying accountable to your vision of Financial Freedom.

Let me share a story with you about just how this can work in real life.

Kyle was a business consultant with over 25 years of experience in his field, while Megan was an elementary school teacher. They wanted more than anything to achieve Financial Freedom within the next 10 years, but didn't know where to start.

When they came to see me, the first thing I did was take them through the exercises we laid out in this chapter. What they came up with was the following: Financial Freedom meant that Kyle would be able to cut his practice in half within the next 10 years, and that Megan could retire within the next five years.

This would allow Megan more time to volunteer at her church and visit her daughter, who would soon be going to college, while Kyle could pursue starting another business venture.

We wrote this down as a vision statement, and they began reviewing and reflecting on it each day so that, when any question was presented to them regarding how they spent their time or their wealth, they could ask themselves: "Will our decision align with our vision statement?" If it would, they felt good about it; if it wouldn't, they moved on. An additional benefit of this process was that it helped create a greater sense of excitement and belief in their vision, which gave them the additional motivation they needed to fuel the right actions and maintain them long enough to begin making real progress on their goals.

So, this simple process, along with their discipline and hard work, allowed Kyle and Megan to reach their destination. Today, they are enjoying the Financial Freedom that seemed unreachable only a few years ago. And the same can happen for you.

Key Takeaways

- Define what Financial Freedom means specifically for you.

- Translate your unique definition of Financial Freedom into an empowering vision statement.

- Focus your mindset around that vision statement and use it as your guiding star for present financial decisions.

FINANCIAL FREEDOM VISION PAGE

Financial Freedom means that I can

_____

without regard to the income it provides so that

I can pursue the following things that fill me

with joy, purpose, and passion:

_____,

_____,

and

_____.

*Plans fail for lack of counsel, but with
many advisors they succeed.*

PROVERBS 15:22 (NIV)

*Alone we can do so little;
together we can do so much.*

HELEN KELLER

CHAPTER 2

ASSEMBLING YOUR FINANCIAL DREAM TEAM

The 1992 Olympics in Barcelona were the first Games that permitted professional basketball players to compete, after the International Basketball Federation voted to change its rules that stipulated that only amateurs could represent their countries at the Olympics. This led to the forming of the legendary U.S. "Dream Team" stacked with top NBA players, including Michael Jordan, Scottie Pippen, Magic Johnson, Larry Bird, Patrick Ewing, and Charles Barkley. Unsurprisingly, this squad utterly dominated the competition, outscoring its opponents by an average of 44 points a game and going undefeated en route to the gold medal.

When it comes to your Financial Freedom, I want the same for you: your very own squad of financial experts, each using their individual specialties in tandem with their other team members to help you achieve your wealth goals. This chapter will show you who needs to be on your team, and how to build one that can help you take the necessary actions to achieve your goals.

Drafting Your Financial Dream Team

First off, we need to note that everyone's personal Dream Team will be a little different, as different situations and goals may require you to bring on experts with different kinds of specialties. However, the most fundamental players on your team will typically include:

- a financial advisor,
- a tax expert,
- an estate attorney, and
- an insurance specialist.

Let's take a brief look at each of these roles, and why they are critical to the success of your plan.

Financial Advisor

The function of your financial advisor is to help you develop a comprehensive and effective plan that will help you achieve your goals. They will help you understand exactly where you are and where you want to go financially, so that they can then give you advice on how best to bridge this gap. While advisors typically help you develop an investment strategy that fits you and your goals, some will go beyond just your investments and work to coordinate all the pieces of your financial plan, to ensure that all are completed.

Tax Expert

A tax expert's function is to help you minimize the tax drag on your income and investment returns. Their primary role may be to help you with your returns each year, identifying ways to reduce your tax burden without reducing your cash flow. The best ones may also be consultants on any financial transaction impacting your taxes. In these ways, their expert advice can help you keep more of what you earn, allowing you to make quicker progress on your goals.

Estate Attorney

An estate attorney's role is to help you draft the necessary legal documents (such as a will, a trust, and power of attorney documents) to ensure that your assets are passed on to the people and organizations that are most meaningful to you. They can also help you reduce the potential tax impact on your estate as it passes to the next generation, so that you can have the comfort of knowing that your family will be taken care of.

Insurance Specialist

The role of an insurance specialist is risk management. They can help you identify the biggest risks to your plan, and find the right amount of coverage to protect you against them. This coverage will come in many different forms, but its ultimate goal is to prevent any of these risks from slowing down your progress towards achieving your Financial Freedom goals by protecting the wealth and cash flow you have worked so hard to build.

As I noted above, your team may also require other players. For example, if you are a real estate investor, you will need a realtor and mortgage banker. Or, if you're a small business owner, you will need the help of a commercial lending expert. And if you're a corporate executive, you will need a specialist to help you maximize the benefits of your various employer retirement and stock plans.

Whatever your situation, though, you need to make sure that your team fits both where you are right now financially, and where you want to be heading. If you are uncertain of exactly who should be on your financial team, then your financial advisor could be a great resource for you, as they have put together your plan and evaluated your complete wealth picture. In addition, they also may be able to directly introduce you to the specific professionals you need on your team.

Finding Your Money Mentor

Now that you have a better idea of the financial professionals you need, the next step is to identify the right person to lead your Dream Team—what I call your Money Mentor. This role is summarized quite well by a saying of Ralph Waldo Emerson's: "Our chief want in life is somebody who shall make us do what we can." This is what your Money Mentor is there for: to help you harness and direct your own power and potential to help you reach your Financial Freedom goals.

Your Money Mentor will work to ensure that all the pieces of your plan are in place, and that your team members are working together efficiently. They will be a coach, designing a game plan and showing you what you need to execute it. They will be a cheerleader, praising your progress and encouraging you to keep going on your wealth journey in the face of obstacles or challenges. Sometimes, they may need to be a drill sergeant, getting in your face and holding you accountable to your plan when you start putting obstacles in your own way (like when you would rather buy a bigger house with a larger mortgage instead of putting that money towards your retirement plan). And they can also play the role of wise counselor, using the benefits of their experience to give you perspective on the bigger picture and help you avoid making mistakes that could derail your plan (such as helping you see the benefits of maintaining your investment strategy in a down market, or reminding you to keep your wealth protected from risks that could set you behind on your goals).

So, where do you find your Money Mentor? They may be one of the financial professionals on your Dream Team, but they don't have to be—it could be someone in your personal life, like a trusted friend or family member. But whoever you choose as your Money Mentor, you will want them to possess the following characteristics:

Competence Your Money Mentor needs to have the fundamental knowledge and ability to give sound advice regarding your wealth. Whether they're a financial expert themselves, or someone you know who has managed and stewarded their wealth in the same ways you would like to do, you will need to confidently determine that they know what they're talking about when it comes to money.

A word of caution here: your Money Mentor should be someone you can trust to share the details of your financial life with and be certain that they will remain confidential. This can be a stumbling block for people who choose a family member or friend: sometimes, the person seeking advice doesn't want to share with them the full details of their financial situation, for fear of being embarrassed or ashamed in front of someone who's close to them. But if you're not willing to be fully transparent with your Money Mentor, your success will be limited at best.

For this reason, people will often seek out a financial professional as their Money Mentor. But it shouldn't just be the first name you see in the phone book, of course. Ideally, you would get an introduction to them from someone you know and trust, who can recommend their services.

With or without that, though, you should answer a few important questions about anyone you're considering to be your Money Mentor:

- How long have they been in business?

- What professional designations do they have?

- What experience do they have in helping others like you achieve their goals?

- Does their way of managing wealth line up with yours?

- How much will it cost to work with them?

- Do they plan to continue their work long enough to help you make it to your goals?

Connection Your Money Mentor should be someone you connect with and relate to easily, who you like to be around and talk to. There will be many deep, and sometimes difficult, conversations that you'll be having with them over the course of your wealth journey, so you need to be comfortable in your interactions with them.

You may already have this relationship in place if you've chosen a friend or family member as your Money Mentor. If you're seeking a financial profes-sional for this role, however, you'll have to determine whether or not you can develop this kind of rapport. This is why it's wise to have an initial consultation with a potential professional Money Mentor before you start working with them. If the connection is there, then you can set about embarking on your journey with them; if it isn't, then you should keep looking.

Caring You should know for a fact that your Money Mentor has your back and wants you to succeed. Their actions and attitude should all speak to how, when it comes to your Financial Freedom, your needs are their priority—that they'll always be there for you when you need them, and that you can always count on them to push you in the right direction.

Candid You need to know that your Money Mentor will be sincere, honest, and direct with you. They will always tell you what you need to hear, even when it may be uncomfortable. In return for that promise of candidness, you need to commit to a few responsibilities as well:

- You must be able to receive input from your Money Mentor without getting combative or defensive. This can be difficult, because sometimes what's best for you goes against what you want at the moment.

- You must always be transparent about your financial situation with your Money Mentor. If you ask your mentor what you should do in a given financial situation, but deliberately withhold an accurate picture of your balance sheet, there is no way that they can give you the advice you need.

- You need to demonstrate a willingness to put their advice into action. If you don't heed their advice consistently, they may feel like the investment of their time and energy into this relationship is not worth it for them. You would then lose your mentor and have to start the process of finding one again—which, obviously, could delay your progress towards your goals.

Your Money Mentor is a central figure in your plan, and finding and keeping the right person in this role is one of the most important decisions that you will make. They are the glue that will keep your Dream Team working together effectively as you devise your game plan for achieving Financial Freedom.

Drawing Up Your Game Plan

So, you've identified your Money Mentor, and you know who needs to be on your Dream Team. All your players are now in place, which means that the next step is implementing a process for getting them to work together effectively. There's no point in getting the most skilled players out onto the court if their skills don't complement each other, and if they're not all working in harmony towards the same goal.

Here's an example of how different kinds of professional expertise can complement each other. Jason and Heather came in to review their investment portfolio with me, and told me that they had read an article about how they could create some tax-free income when they retired. During our conversation, I told them they could achieve this goal by converting some of their current retirement accounts to a Roth IRA. Still, I warned them that the conversion amount would become immediately taxable in that tax year. Based on this conversion, they thought it was something they would like to do. But, before we moved forward with it, I had us connect with their tax specialist so that they knew exactly what their tax liability would be.

At our meeting, the tax specialist ran a few different examples for Jason and Heather about how much tax liability would be created should they convert some of their traditional IRAs to Roth IRAs. It surprised them how much it would cost to convert the amount they had initially planned. So, because of this consultation, they decided to convert less than their original target, which saved them a considerable amount in taxes that year even as they were still able to begin the process of building some tax-free income for their retirement.

As you can see, keeping the lines of communication among your team members open is highly important to your plan's success. This can be done in a couple of different ways.

One method is for your Money Mentor to join you for meetings with the other professionals on your team. Since they have a detailed understanding of your plan and what needs to be done, they can make sure that everyone is on the same page. Your Money Mentor could then send a summary email of any action items so that everyone is updated on any changes to your plan.

For more complex updates or decisions, it can be helpful to gather all your team members in the same place to review your plan. Your Money Mentor can facilitate the conversation, making sure all the relevant items are discussed and decided upon with the bigger picture of your plan in view.

In this chapter, we've covered how to go about identifying and assembling the experts you need for your

Financial Dream Team, and the qualities needed for the Money Mentor who will lead and coordinate the team's efforts. Now, it's time to take the true first step on your Financial Freedom journey, which, for many, can often be the most frightening—namely, determining exactly how far away you are from the goal you want to reach. It can seem daunting or dispiriting to see the distance you have to travel to reach Financial Freedom, but, as you'll see in the next chapter, finding out the true extent of that distance is your first step in conquering it.

Key Takeaways

- Assemble a Dream Team of financial professionals tailored to your situation and Financial Freedom goals.

- Select a Money Mentor whose experience and advice you trust to lead your Dream Team.

- Ensure open lines of communication among your Dream Team members to keep everyone aligned.

For which of you, desiring to build a tower,
does not first sit down and count the cost,
whether he has enough to complete it?
Luke 14:28

If we could first know where we are, and
whither we are tending, we could then
better judge what to do, and how to do it.
ABRAHAM LINCOLN

CHAPTER 3

BRIDGING YOUR GOAL GAP

could hear the anxiety in Christopher and Ashley's voices as our meeting began. They were in careers that they once loved, but had now determined that they wanted to be free of them within the next 10 years. But they were very uncertain if they could accomplish this, let alone be able to help their three kids pay for college over that same period. These goals were daunting enough on their own, but were overwhelming when combined.

Throughout our first meeting, a couple of things became abundantly clear. Firstly, each of them had a strong work ethic, and neither would shy away from taking the necessary steps towards their goals; they just needed clarification and confidence as to what those steps should be. Secondly, the root cause of their anxiety was that they didn't know at that moment where they were in relationship to either of their primary wealth goals. They felt blind to their financial situation, and, this being the case, they had imagined the worst—that they would have to work at least another 20 years before they could stop.

You may feel like you're in a similar position as Christopher and Ashley, not knowing where you are in relation to your most important financial goals. But, having completed Chapter 1, you've already formulated your vision statement about what Financial Freedom looks like to you and established your major goals. Now, all you need to do is get a clearer picture of how much those goals will cost; and then, how that number compares to your current financial position. The difference between these two points is your *goal gap*—the distance you will have to bridge to reach your goals.

Even though that number may look daunting, believe me—simply getting a reasonably accurate picture of how far your journey will be goes a long way towards reducing your stress and uncertainty, and it can spur you into creating an effective plan for getting there. This is what we will cover in this chapter.

Determine the Cost of Your Goals

As I said above, the first step in bridging your goal gap is knowing how much each of your Financial Freedom goals will cost. To illustrate this process, let's look at the five steps I walked Christopher and Ashley through to estimate how much portfolio value they would need for their goal of Financial Freedom.

1. **Estimate the annual spending income needed to fund your Financial Freedom lifestyle.** Create what you want your Financial Freedom budget to look like when you stop working, including fun items such as travel and hobbies, and not-so-fun items like medical costs and insurance. Factor in any debts that would be paid off by that time, like your mortgage, as that will reduce what income you would need to support your lifestyle. You can also estimate this figure by using your current take-home income as a starting point. For Christopher and Ashley, the spending income they knew they needed to fund their Financial Freedom lifestyle was $100,000 per year.

2. **State the desired timeframe in years you want to achieve this goal.** In Christopher and Ashley's case, they wanted to achieve Financial Freedom within the next 10 years.

3. **Adjust your estimated annual Financial Freedom spending income for inflation.** This is necessary to be able to maintain your purchasing power as prices of goods and services increase over time. So, using the average inflation rate of 3.10%,[2] Christopher and Ashley's goal of retiring in 10 years on an annual budget of $100,000 meant that they would have to adjust that figure to roughly $135,000

to maintain their desired spending power. You can make your own calculation using this tool,[3] or a financial calculator.

4. **Modify your inflation-adjusted income for taxes.** To do this, you will need to estimate your tax burden when you stop working. This can be challenging, because tax rates can be difficult to predict. In Christopher and Ashley's case, they assumed that the rate in 10 years would be at least where it was currently, at about 20%. Factoring in that rate, they determined that they would need to create a gross annual income of $168,750[4] to achieve their Financial Freedom lifestyle.

5. **Subtract any known income sources you will receive when you stop working from your gross annual income.** This could include pensions, Social Security benefits, rental income, or any other source of passive income you know you will be able to benefit from. You can also subtract any active (working) income if your idea of Financial Freedom involves shifting to a different type of work than what you're currently doing.

   Christopher and Ashley's 10-year timeline meant that they would be 62 by the time they hit their Financial Freedom target. This meant that they would have some Social Security income, but neither would have any pensions.

If they decided to take their Social Security at age 62, they estimated that their combined benefits would be about $40,000 per year, based on their most recent benefit report from Social Security.

As their idea of Financial Freedom was to not have to work, this means that they would not have any active (working) income when they retired. However, they did own a few rental properties that they intended to keep, which they estimated would provide them with an annual income of $25,000. So, subtracting this annual rental income, along with their projected Social Security benefits at age 62, from their gross annual income target of $168,750, they determined that their investment portfolio would need to generate $103,750 per year ($168,750, less $25,000, less $40,000) to support their Financial Freedom lifestyle.

How much can I withdraw from my portfolio?

After completing these five steps, there was one final thing that Christopher and Ashley had to do: estimate the portfolio value they would need in 10 years to fund this annual income amount. This can be challenging, because one of the main variables required to make this calculation is a reasonable estimate of how long that income would be needed. In other words, how long do you, or you and your partner, need that portfolio income to support your Financial Freedom goals?

For Christopher and Ashley, since they planned to reach Financial Freedom by age 62, that length of time could easily be 25 years or more. This meant that they would need to be mindful of how much they withdrew from their portfolio each year—as, if they pulled out too much too early, this would put them at risk of running out of money before they ran out of life. Not a great place to be!

So, working from that baseline, the question is: What is a sustainable withdrawal rate for a portfolio that needs to last for 25 years or more?

There are different schools of thought on this question, and many books have been written on the topic. But ultimately, of course, the decision is up to you—after all, it's your money, and only you can control how much you spend each year. That said, the annual withdrawal rate that I've seen used most often is in the range of 3% to 5% of the portfolio value. If you want to play it safer, or plan to stop working at a younger age and thus will need your portfolio to generate income for a longer period, you will want to stay on the lower end of this range.

How much money do I really need?

Once you've decided which rate best suits you and your situation, you have just one more calculation to make: dividing your annual portfolio income by your planned annual withdrawal rate to determine the overall portfolio value you will need to fund your lifestyle.

As we saw above, the annual gross income that Christopher and Ashley needed to fund their Financial Freedom lifestyle was $103,750. They decided that they wanted to be more conservative with the withdrawal rate from their portfolio, and thus pegged it at 3%. By dividing their annual gross income by their chosen annual withdrawal rate, they determined that they would need about $3,458,000[5] of overall portfolio value to reach their goal.

Determine Your Current Financial Position

You've now determined the first point of your goal gap—that is, how much your goals will cost in portfolio value. The next step is to get an accurate picture of your financial state as it stands now.

To do this, you will need to create or update your personal balance sheet. At the back of this book, you'll find a balance sheet worksheet to help you do this. To complete it, you will need to gather the following information:

1. Bank statements for both savings and checking

2. Brokerage or investment account statements

3. College savings account, educational IRA, or custodial account statements

4. Employer plan statements, such as 401ks, 403bs, and profit-sharing plans

5. Your traditional IRA and/or Roth IRA statements

6. Estimated values for your primary residence and other real estate holdings, such as vacation or investment property

7. Estimated values of any business ownership positions (your own or others)

8. Your most recent tax return

On the worksheet, you will fill in the approximate value for each asset. Then, in the space next to each asset, you will designate the goal that asset will need to fund.

For some of these assets, those goals will be straightforward—for example, employer retirement plans, or college savings accounts and any college goals you may have for your family. Others may not be quite so clear, or may have multiple designations. For instance, you may have an investment account that you may use to fund the purchase of a second home, but if not used for that purpose would be used for your Financial Freedom goal. In these cases, just do your best to assign a specific goal to each account; you can always go back and adjust them later.

Finding Your Goal Gap

Once you've completed the worksheet, you're ready for the final step: comparing the cost of each of your Financial Freedom goals to the current balances of the accounts designated to fund those goals. Let's turn back to Christopher and Ashley's 10-year Financial Freedom plan to show how this works.

As we saw above, Christopher and Ashley determined that they would need about $3.458 million to fund their Financial Freedom lifestyle. Then, using the steps to build their balance sheet, they discovered that they currently had $1.5 million allocated to the funds they had designated for their Financial Freedom plan. Their goal gap was thus the difference between $3.458 million and $1.5 million, which is $1.958 million.

While this felt like a big number for them to hit within the next 10 years, now they at least knew the target they were aiming at. With that locked in, we could begin creating an effective plan for them to close the gap in their chosen timeline.

It's important to note that Christopher and Ashley had by no means finalized their Financial Freedom plan by this point. However, completing these steps did give them greater confidence about their ultimate success, and the impetus to begin taking the sustained action to get there. Their change in demeanor at the end of this process was palpable: they had started out completely in the dark, paralyzed into inaction with the fear that they would not be able to achieve their financial objectives. Now, with greater clarity about how far they actually had to go, they could begin moving forward—which is precisely what they did, by immediately increasing their annual contributions to their retirement plans and rebalancing the investment strategy to fit them and their Financial Freedom goals.

By completing the worksheet included with this book, you can discover the width of your goal gap, which means that you're one step closer to building an investment plan that is custom-fit for you and your unique vision of Financial Freedom.

Key Takeaways

- Estimate the cost of your Financial Freedom goals based on such factors as timeframe, inflation, taxes, and income sources.

- Determine the portfolio value and withdrawal rate you will require to fund your goals.

- Perform a thorough assessment of your current financial situation.

- Calculate your "goal gap" through the difference between your current financial situation and the estimated costs of your Financial Freedom goals.

*If you can find a path with no obstacles,
it probably doesn't lead anywhere.*

FRANK A. CLARK

CHAPTER 4

WHAT ARE THE OBSTACLES IN YOUR PATH TO FINANCIAL FREEDOM?

ake no mistake: there are unique obstacles that Generation X will face on their Financial Freedom journey that will make it more challenging for them to achieve their goals than any previous generation. And the bigger those goals are, the greater the obstacles are likely to be.

But now, the good news: knowing what these obstacles are, and how they will or may impact you, can help you create a plan for addressing them. This foreknowledge may help reduce your fear and anxiety about these obstacles, and thus potentially increase your ability to push past them. In this chapter, we will cover the four major obstacles on your path to Financial Freedom; how they can combine to pose a bigger threat than they do individually; and ideas you can use to mitigate and help overcome these challenges.

The Four Obstacles
to Financial Freedom

The four major obstacles you are likely to encounter on your Financial Freedom journey are:

- Longevity

- Inflation

- Income insecurity

- Competing priorities

Let's look at each of these in turn.

1. Longevity

Generation X could live longer than any previous generation of retirees. You'd think that would be a blessing, not an obstacle, right? Well, the fact is, it's both.

The downside of living a longer life is that your money must provide for you and your family for longer than any previous generation, due to two interrelated factors:

i. The average life expectancy for someone turning 65 in 2016 was to live for another 20 years. This is about six years longer than someone who turned 65 in 1960.[6]

ii. People are retiring earlier than previous generations. The average retirement age in 2010 was 64.[7]

Put together, these two factors create an obstacle for both Generation X and the generations that come after it, as they may only be amplified as time goes on.

The risk here, obviously, is that you may run out of money before you run out of life. If this were to happen, it would most likely find you at a point where you would neither want nor be able to return to work, and would thus have to significantly reduce your lifestyle or require the assistance of others, such as your children. In my years as a financial advisor, I've never met anyone who thought either of those options was a good fallback plan.

So then, the question is: How long will Generation X need to plan for their assets to fund their Financial Freedom lifestyle?

Earlier generations typically worked as long as their health allowed before they retired, meaning that many of them spent 10 years or less in retirement and typically lived on their Social Security benefits and/or a pension, rather than their assets. For Generation X, conversely, it's not outside the realm of possibility that many will spend as many years in retirement as they did working, and possibly even longer. This could mean 30 years or more that you will need your assets to provide for your lifestyle—which, it's obvious to see, is a lot more challenging to plan for than 10 years or less.

2. Inflation

The products and services that we need and want become more expensive over time, which means that our purchasing power is gradually reduced. Put another way, we will need more income in the future just to maintain the standard of living that we enjoy today.

What does this mean for your Financial Freedom goals? As we noted in the previous chapter, the long-term inflation rate in the United States averages about 3%, which would mean that your income needs to roughly double every 24 years just to maintain, not increase, your current standard of living. So, if the period of your Financial Freedom will be 30 years or more, your income at the end of this time period would need to be more than twice what it was at the beginning.

If your income can't keep up with these increases, you may have to reduce your lifestyle; take a larger amount out of your portfolio each year; or return to working in some capacity, if you are able and willing. But, assuming that you have no wish to rejoin the workforce, we can firmly say that none of these is a great option.

Inflation is a stealth enemy. In the short run, it can have little to no impact on your wealth, but over 20 or 30 years it can deteriorate your Financial Freedom plan by reducing your purchasing power, your principal, or both. This is especially true for those retirees who do not maintain enough potential for growth on their investments once they retire. Consider the case below.

Paul and Mary retired and invested their nest egg of $1 million in a fixed investment that paid them a set interest rate of 3% for 20 years. This equated to an income of $30,000 per year, which they used to help fund their lifestyle. In the beginning, everything worked fine for them, but as the years passed they noticed flaws in their investment approach. Specifically, the cost of their lifestyle had almost doubled in the 20 years that they had retired, but their portfolio income had not.

To make matters even worse, the principal value of their investments had not grown over the years, as they had pulled all of the interest out for living expenses. So, at the end of 20 years, their principal investment had remained at $1 million, which is exactly what they started retirement with. They were now faced with a very challenging decision: Would they reduce their lifestyle to fit their income? Or would they begin drawing from their principal to maintain it?

Neither seemed like a good option to them, so they looked for an alternative solution, which we will talk more about in Chapter 7. What's important to understand at this point, however, is that longevity plus inflation may equal disaster if your Financial Freedom plan has not accounted for it.

3. Income insecurity

Historically, the two plans that have provided a fixed monthly income for life to people in retirement are Social Security and company pension plans. This system was secure and effective for retirees, because:

a. it was based on the guarantees of either the government or their former employer;

b. more people contributed to the plans than were withdrawing from them, allowing these funds to continue to build even as withdrawals were coming out; and

c. people generally lived shorter lives, putting less pressure on these plans to make payments.

These factors no longer hold, as fewer people contribute to these plans while more people are living longer in their retirement years than ever. The result is that fewer people will be able to enjoy a retirement pension, as there are not as many plans existing now as there were just a generation ago.

Let's crunch some numbers to help illustrate this. The percentage of private wage and salary workers covered by a defined benefit pension plan has declined from 38% in 1980 to just 20% in 2008. This according to a 2008 study by the Bureau of Labor Statistics. The viability of the Social Security trust fund's ability to pay out full benefits has also been called into question, which creates some uncertainty around this being there in its current form to Generation X and younger generations.

Based on the 2024 Social Security trust fund report, the surplus reserves used to pay out benefits will be depleted in 2034, one year earlier than reported in the previous year's report. At that point, its ability to pay benefits will be based solely on what it takes each year in the form of Social Security taxes, which would reduce benefits to payees to around 77% of their projected benefits.[8] This depletion and reduction of benefits would roughly coincide with when Generation X becomes eligible to receive these payments.

So, what impact will it have on Generation X and future generations if neither of these programs exists as they did before? Should people even use it when planning for their retirement? The answers to these two questions—which will differ on a case-by-case basis—will tremendously affect their planning. However, if we go by the report above, there will most likely be Social Security benefits for Generation X, but in a reduced form—something about 23% lower—if no changes are made to the program.[9]

Let's look at a test case to paint the picture in even more detail.

John, age 50, would like to reach his Financial Freedom goals by 62, and will not have a pension plan available to him. His Social Security benefit at 62 is projected to be $2,500 per month, and he has contributed to his employer plans and has some investment accounts. However, he is uncertain about the future viability of the Social Security program, and so wants to know: "Will I have enough to provide for my needed income if no Social Security is available?"

To answer this, we will need to figure out how much more John will need to accumulate in assets to make up for the gap if his promised Social Security benefit does not materialize. Assuming that his investment portfolio could generate a 4% annual withdrawal rate, John would need at least an additional $750,000 extra in his investment accounts to make up for the hypothetical Social Security shortfall.[10]

To clarify, at this point we don't know with any certainty that neither of these programs will be available for Generation X. There are still some pension plans out there, and, for the present moment, Social Security will likely still be in place in some form when Gen X begins to hit retirement age. However, it is probably best to plan for the worst. This means that, if you don't factor Social Security into your Financial Freedom plan and the program is still in place by the time you retire, you'll have more income than you expected. Nothing wrong with that!

4. **Competing priorities**

In general, there are three competing priorities Gen Xers may face while pursuing Financial Freedom:

i.   Growing their portfolio to fund their Financial Freedom plan.

ii. Providing medical expenses and care for aging parents.

iii. Funding the educational costs of their children.

We've already extensively discussed the first of these, and there's more to come—after all, it's the subject of the whole book! So let's take a look at the second two priorities to see how they could impact your planning.

Helping aging parents Although we may need to assist our aging parents in a variety of ways, such as running errands or taking them to doctor's appointments, the primary financial expenses will typically be related to health care costs. And, if they're not planned for, these costs could be expensive, depending on the level of care required.

This factor could impact your Financial Freedom plan by requiring that you reallocate funds intended for your savings towards care costs, and/or potentially necessitate that you take time away from work to assist your parents, which means that you would be earning less money and thus have less to direct towards your financial goals. To be clear, I'm in no way trying to discourage you from properly caring for your parents—my point is simply that attaining your wealth goals can be more challenging if you find yourself in this situation.

Educational funding If you think you will have to care for your aging parents while simultaneously putting your children through college, you are officially part of what is called the "sandwich generation"—and that sandwich is far from tasty.

It should come as no surprise to hear that college costs have jumped dramatically over the last few decades. In the 2004 school year, the average cost of a four-year undergraduate degree was around $48,000 for out-of-state tuition for a public university, and $80,000 for a private university. Over the next 20 years, those tuition amounts jumped to around $113,000 and $187,000, respectively—that's approximately 2.5 times higher over that timeframe.[11] Talk about inflation!

The fact is that if you want to fund all or most of those costs for your children, then they need to be factored into your Financial Freedom plan accordingly.

Knowledge is Power

My purpose in this chapter was not to make you fearful of the obstacles that may lie in your way on your journey to Financial Freedom. Rather, it was to heighten your awareness of these obstacles and the impact they could have on your planning, and, by knowing this, provide you with the inspiration, intensity, and determination to push through those obstacles. I firmly believe that, when it comes to achieving your Financial Freedom, knowledge is power—and, when it combines with your vision and your desire to make that vision a reality, it makes for a pretty mighty engine.

All right. We now know how far we are from our Financial Freedom goals, and the obstacles we could potentially face along the way. Next, it's time to learn about and take stock of the tools that can help us on our journey—the investment strategies and principles you can use to start creating your Financial Freedom strategy to help carry you towards your goals.

Key Takeaways

- Identify and address the four main obstacles to Financial Freedom: longevity, inflation, income insecurity, and competing priorities.

- Recognize that these obstacles can combine to pose an even greater threat when considered together.

- Understand the obstacles between you and your Financial Freedom goals to diminish fear and proactively lessen their impact.

PART 2

STRATEGIES DESIGNED FOR REACHING FINANCIAL FREEDOM

*Look at market fluctuations as your friend
rather than your enemy; profit from folly
rather than participate in it.*

WARREN BUFFETT

CHAPTER 5

INVESTMENT PRINCIPLES

I hardly need to remind you of the tumultuous start to 2020 due to the global outbreak of coronavirus. The S&P 500 Index's response to the pandemic was to pull back; at one point in March, it had lost over 30% of its value from its high earlier in the year. This naturally caused angst for investors, as they watched their investment portfolios plummet as the world shut down.

One of those investors was Troy. He had been getting closer to reaching his Financial Freedom goal, and so began looking for additional information about what to do in response to this pullback. But the more news he watched and read only served to create more fear and confusion instead of helping him decide what to do. He began checking his account values online multiple times a day, which also did not help calm his nerves. In addition, he began talking to everybody he worked with about what he was seeing and feeling about his investment accounts. Hearing their own fears and anxieties in response created a negative feedback loop that left him paralyzed by uncertainty and inaction.

In desperation, Troy finally decided to eliminate what was causing him all this anxiety: his investment portfolio's allocation to risky investments, such as stocks. So, he called his advisor and liquidated his entire portfolio to cash. Unfortunately, he did this right before the market began recovering—meaning that he had experienced all the downside of the market pullback, but no benefits from its bounce back.

Many of us can relate to stories like Troy's, especially the fear that drove him to make his fateful decision. That's why this chapter will be dedicated to teaching you how to control that fear by adhering to key principles that investors such as Warren Buffett have used to survive, and sometimes even thrive, during chaotic markets. Learning these principles and sticking to them can help you calm your nerves during times of trial, and give you the time necessary to work towards investment success by focusing on what you can control (your mindset and actions) and successfully navigating the things you can't (the world and the markets).

Before we delve into those principles, though, we're going to go over the first two steps you should take when facing difficult markets.

How to Face Difficult Market Conditions

The first step is to refer back to the Financial Freedom plan that you created in advance of this challenging situation, and evaluate whether or not your investment strategy still fits you and your goals. In addition to that future focus, you should also evaluate how much downward movement you can handle in your portfolio without losing sleep or reducing your quality of life— because even if your plan still fits your goals, it may not fit in terms of your current situation or comfort level with market risk. And, if your investment allocation does not fit you correctly, then it's probably not sustainable.

If, after careful review, you conclude that your plan still does fit both your goals and your present situation, then it's likely that no major changes are warranted, even though you may feel like you should do *something* in response to what you're seeing in the news or on your investment statements. The greater your ability to stay true to your investment allocation plan during challenging times, the more likely you are to potentially achieve your goals over the long haul.

And remember, you're not alone in this. You can find that fortitude with the support of the Financial Dream Team you've assembled, regularly reviewing your portfolio with your Money Mentor or financial advisor. I often tell my clients, "I can't promise you that your investments will never go down in value, but I can promise you that when they do, I will be right alongside you to help guide you through the storm."

The second initial step to take during seasons of turmoil in the markets is to test your plan for its long-term success rate. This testing can be done in different ways. Personally, I've always found it most beneficial to use a financial planning tool that takes the details of my clients' Financial Freedom plan and current financial situation, such as their goals, the time horizons for reaching these goals, their cash flow, and their current asset levels; tests their plan across a range of possible outcomes; and then provides an estimated success rate for their plan. Whether the tool shows them that they are still on target to reach their goals despite their reduced account values due to the market pullback, or if that pullback has thrown them off target, they can determine the actions they need to take because they now know exactly where they stand.

The reality is that there will always be something to worry about when it comes to your investment strategy. It could be a virus, a geopolitical event, an election, a public policy announcement, or anything else that rattles markets and investors' nerves. Times like these are when emotions run high, and can make your thinking (and portfolio allocation) go off track.

This is where your financial plan can be of tremendous value. It can help you filter through all the noise and refocus you on your values, goals, and intentions. It is your Financial Freedom plan, not the headlines of the day, that should be the most significant driver of any changes you make to your portfolio. Your plan is designed purposefully and intentionally so that, like a map, it can guide you to your desired destination, even when times get tough.

Now that you've taken those first two "deep breaths," we can look at how to apply the seven key investment principles that can help you on your Financial Freedom journey.

PRINCIPLE #1: Diversification matters

You've surely heard the old adage, "Don't put all your eggs in one basket." That's the essence of diversification. It's a risk management approach that seeks to reduce the potential of loss to your portfolio by spreading your investments around strategically, so that you don't lose everything or nearly everything if one of them fails.

The risks to your portfolio are multiple. A few common ones are:

- *Market risk.* Affects the performance of the overall market. Market risk may arise due to changes to interest rates, exchange rates, geopolitical events, or recessions. Market risk can be reduced, but not eliminated, through diversification.

- *Interest risk.* Changes in overall interest rates affect your returns and yield, especially on fixed income investments like bonds. As interest rates rise, bond prices fall, and vice versa. Interest rate risk can be reduced through diversification of bond maturities.

- *Inflation risk.* The risk that rising prices will undermine an investment's returns through a decline in their purchasing power.

- *Geographical risk.* The ways in which changes in the economy of another country impact your returns.

You can use different asset classes to mitigate these risks by diversifying and blending them together in such a way as to help achieve your ideal risk-return combinations. For example, you may use stocks to offset inflation risk; bonds to reduce stock market risk; and stocks of multiple countries to reduce your geographic risk.

Generally, the more volatility you can or are willing to accept, the greater your potential for returns. This trade-off is summarized in the chart below, which is commonly known as the *Efficient Frontier*.

There are many asset classes that can be used in the diversification process, but the most common ones are:

- stocks,

- bonds,

- cash, and

- real estate.

It is important to get your blending of these various assets correct, because this will be a critical factor in determining your portfolio returns over time and will determine the level of volatility you are willing to accept for these returns. In my opinion, the latter factor is just as important as the former, because if your risk surpasses the level you can handle (either materially or mentally), you will be more likely to panic and veer away from your Financial Freedom plan.

BAIRD

Diversification can lead to better risk/return trade-offs

The Efficient Frontier

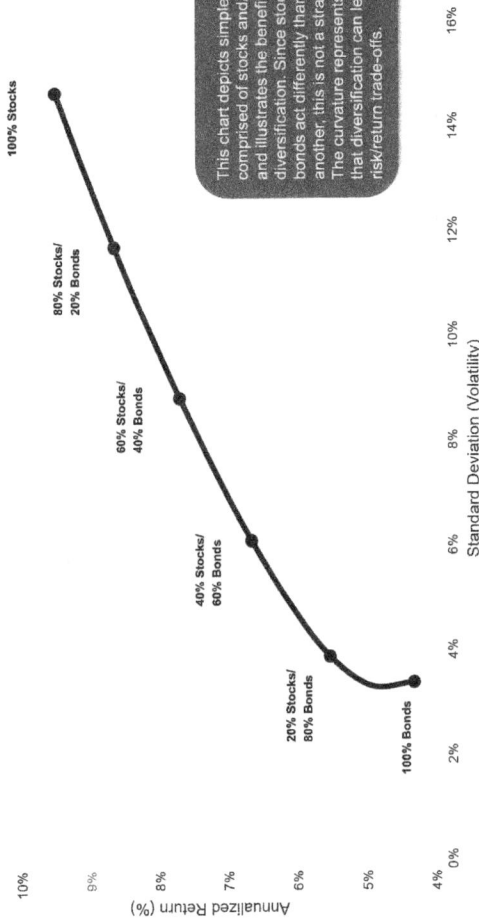

Annualized Return (%)

100% Stocks

80% Stocks/
20% Bonds

60% Stocks/
40% Bonds

40% Stocks/
60% Bonds

20% Stocks/
80% Bonds

100% Bonds

Standard Deviation (Volatility)

10%
9%
8%
7%
6%
5%
4%

0%   2%   4%   6%   8%   10%   12%   14%   16%

This chart depicts simple portfolios comprised of stocks and/or bonds and illustrates the benefits of diversification. Since stocks and bonds act differently than one another, this is not a straight line. The curvature represents the fact that diversification can lead to better risk/return trade-offs.

Source: Standard and Poor's, Barclays. For the 20-year period ending December 31, 2023. Stocks are represented by the S&P 500 Index, bonds by the Barclays Aggregate Bonds Index. The S&P 500 Index is a well-known gauge of stock market movements determined by the weighted capitalization of the 500 leading U.S. common stocks. The Barclays Aggregate Bond Index is a broad U.S. bond benchmark composed of Treasury, government-related, corporate and securitized bonds. It includes investment-grade securities that have at least one year to maturity and an outstanding par value of at least $250 million. These allocations were rebalanced monthly. Indices are unmanaged and are not available for direct investment. Diversification does not guarantee a profit, nor does it ensure against loss. Past performance is not a guarantee of future results. Standard deviation is a statistical measure of performance dispersion. The higher the measure, the more volatile the historical return pattern.

PRINCIPLE #2: Have a margin of safety

Maintaining a margin of safety around your wealth entails building a strategic cash reserve to cover one year or more of living expenses and any major spending items if your portfolio is impacted by negative market fluctuations. For example, if a poor economy or extended market decline causes you to lose your job or income source, that margin of safety will give you a financial cushion to see the crisis through while still sticking to your long-term investment strategy.

Having a few years' worth of planned spending of larger-ticket items set aside gives your investments time to recover before you reach a point where you'd need to pull funds out of them. The longer you can keep your money invested, the better your chances for a positive return on it. The last thing you want to do is have to sell out of your investment portfolio while it is depressed in value. This locks in a loss that cannot be recovered, because the money is no longer invested.

The bottom line is that if you know you will have to spend money on a bigger purchase in the next couple of years, then it is best to leave this money in a more stable type of investment so that you will know that the total value will be available when you need it, even if the return on it is lower. For example, a client of mine likes to take a nice vacation each year, and they have set aside some cash within one of their investment accounts to fund these future trips. This way, when a trip comes up that they would like to take, they don't have to worry about what the market is doing at that time. They know those travel funds are ready and available in their cash reserve account.

"But," you may be asking, "isn't it true that cash doesn't earn as good a return as other investment types? Why should I invest this much of my money in low-returning investments?" The fact is that the interest your cash returns is not the only benefit it can bring to your portfolio. It can also provide value by allowing you to stay invested when markets are ugly, giving your strategy the chance of recovering and possibly reaping the benefits of time in the markets.

PRINCIPLE #3: Expect market volatility, and profit from it

Don't let market downturns surprise or upset you; these are all part of the financial life cycle. Between 1952 and 2021, the S&P 500 Index has lost 10% or more of its value on average about once per year, from which it typically takes 110 days to recover.[12] It has lost 20% or more of its value once every six years, a drop which can require a little over a year to recover. By keeping your cool and not panicking when these downturns inevitably occur, you can seek to profit from them during their subsequent recovery.

There are a couple of ways that expecting these downturns can work to your advantage. The first is relatively passive: namely, by properly accounting and preparing for a down market, you will not be forced into a position where you would have to sell any part of your investment portfolio when one occurs. Doing this may help you to recover lost account value as the market rebounds.

The second is more exciting: it involves not only staying with your investment strategy through a down market, but also adding to it with a portion of the strategic cash reserves that you have built up. This means that you can buy more at discounted prices during the down time, and then hopefully reap long-term rewards as the market recovers.

Remember—to this point, the stock market has always recovered from past corrections, no matter what crisis or tragedy has occurred. Keeping this in mind will not only help calm your nerves during these challenging times, but also give you an edge in accelerating your progress towards your Financial Freedom goals.

PRINCIPLE #4: It's time *in* the market, not the timing *of* the market

Simply put, trying to successfully time the highs and lows of the market is a difficult, if not impossible, task. If you call the market high and sell before it dips, but then fail to re-enter your strategy at the low point before it begins to recover, you will miss some of the gains. The easier path is to find a strategy that works for you and stay in it for the duration.

The chart below illustrates this principle through the performance of the S&P 500 Index over the 10-year period ending December 31, 2021. It shows that if an investor put in $10,000 initially and left it in for that entire period, they would have received the best return. However, if they tried to outguess the market's direction and missed just the best six months of performance, their return would have been cut by almost half. So remember: one of the ways to get the most out of your portfolio is to stay invested over the long haul.

You must be present to win

BAIRD

Missing large market moves impacts wealth creation

growth of $10,000 over 10 years if certain periods are missed

Attempting to time the market's gains or losses is a tricky proposition and can come at a great cost. Missing even one month in the market can impact longer-term results. While ongoing portfolio modifications can be beneficial, large and frequent allocation changes are often detrimental.

Fully Invested	Best 5 days missed	Best 10 days missed	Best 15 days missed	Best 20 days missed
$31,149	$21,608	$17,047	$14,380	$12,368

Source: Standard and Poor's, FactSet, Baird Research. For the 10-year period ending December 31, 2023 (total 120 months). Past performance is not a guarantee of future results. Performance is calculated on a total return basis with dividend reinvestment. The S&P 500, computed by the Standard & Poor's Corporation, is a well known gauge of stock market movements determined by the weighted capitalization of the 500 leading U.S. common stocks. Indices are unmanaged and are not available for direct investment. Past performance is not a guarantee of future results.

PRINCIPLE #5: Understand the dangers of concentration risk

Concentration risk occurs when a large percentage of your investment portfolio is tied up in one stock. It frequently happens in employer plans that provide company-matching and/or profit-sharing contributions directly into the company stock. The issue can be even more pronounced for those employees who receive part of their compensation in stock options—i.e., the opportunity to buy company stock at some point in the future, usually at discounted prices. In situations like these, it is not uncommon for people to have a majority of their retirement portfolio in their company stock.

Of course, this presents no problem if the stock price continues to grow. But unfortunately, that's not always the case. For an extreme example, consider the infamous case of Enron, whose peak stock price of $90.75 a share in August 2000 came crashing down to just $0.26 by December 2001, after revelations of unscrupulous behavior by some of its executives were revealed. A once-strong company was suddenly gone, and it took the retirement accounts of many employees along with it.

So, if more than 10% of your retirement accounts are in your company's stock, you need to ask yourself a few questions. The first is: "Would I be able to achieve my retirement goals if my stock value went to $0 per share?" If the answer is no, you need to consider reducing some of your exposure to the stock.

The second question is: "How comfortable am I having all my current income (in the form of my paycheck) and a considerable amount of my future income (through distributions from my retirement plans) dependent on the health of my current employer?" If that makes you uncomfortable, that's another indication that it may be time to revisit your allocation.

PRINCIPLE #6: Ignore the noise

Limit the amount of financial news you consume. Although it can be very helpful at times, it can also cause you to become overwhelmed as you bounce from station to station, website to website, desperately seeking direction for how to manage your portfolio. Just think about Troy's experience in the example at the beginning of this chapter.

There are two primary reasons that obsessively consuming financial news will likely not give you the answers you need to make the right decisions for your portfolio. The first is that the experts in the media don't know your specific situation, including your goals, risk profile, time horizon, and liquidity needs. Without this, they really are not in the best position to give you the proper advice.

Secondly, financial media's main objective is not to provide you with investment advice customized to your plan, but to push an agenda and/or sell advertising. It seeks to play on your emotions, and may lead you to make bad decisions when markets are at their extremes.

The extremes I'm referring to here are irrational optimism on one side, when stock market returns are going up and up and an investor can seem to do no wrong, and extreme pessimism on the other, when it seems like the sky is falling and the markets may not recover. In either situation, you need to be extremely careful. In times of irrational optimism, greed could cause you to buy investments at the wrong time, when they're overpriced. In times of extreme pessimism, fear can lead you to sell just before the market hits bottom and begins its recovery.

This is why it can be better to consume less news in times of financial crisis, not more. While you do want to stay informed, you also don't want to increase your anxiety and be driven into making poor, reactive decisions.

PRINCIPLE #7: Don't forget to enjoy the moment

There is one final principle that you should adhere to, and it's both simple and challenging. Try to enjoy life in the moment, no matter what the markets and your portfolio are doing. Read a book that brings you enjoyment. Go for a walk and enjoy the sunshine if it's a nice day outside. Or, if you have young kids at home, stop and spend some time with them while doing something they love.

When my daughter was two to three years old, I was going through a challenging season with my business due to difficult market conditions, which led me to focus the bulk of my attention on my financial problems instead of enjoying this season of her life as much as I could have. This remains one of my greatest regrets. The conditions that were causing me stress passed with time, but I could never get back those crucial early years of my daughter's life.

So, I encourage you to never forget to stop and smell the roses, and let the markets work themselves out. That's the whole reason you devised your Financial Freedom plan in the first place, and then shaped your investment strategy to fit it.

Now, it's time to learn how you can do the same thing with your portfolio.

Key Takeaways

- Diversify your portfolio to align with your plan.

- Create a margin of safety for your wealth.

- Expect market volatility and seek to profit from it.

- Focus on time *in* the market rather than trying to time the market.

- Stay cautious of the crowd at market extremes.

- Understand and mitigate concentration risk.

- Ignore market noise; stay focused on your plan.

The investor's chief problem—and even his worst enemy—is likely to be himself.

BENJAMIN GRAHAM

CHAPTER 6

FIND YOUR INVESTMENT FIT

The snow was coming down hard and blowing across the highway, making visibility as bad as I had ever experienced as I drove home after visiting my sister at college. The drive, which in normal conditions should have taken just a few hours, seemed to drag on forever as I inched my way down the road. At some points it was so bad that I was tempted to stop and wait out the storm, but I wanted to get home, so I kept going.

Luckily, the GPS in my car helped me to stay on course despite the storm. And, more than that, it gave me comfort and confidence that I could safely make it back home—which, eventually, I did, to my great relief.

A written investment plan is designed to be like a GPS for your Financial Freedom. It can help you stay on the right path, making progress towards your goals, even when financial storms are happening all around you. By putting your plan down in writing at a time of relative calm, when you can think more clearly about your wealth and what you are trying to accomplish, you can then refer to it in times of stress to keep yourself on course and take your emotions out of the decision-making process, so as to avoid becoming your own worst enemy.

In this chapter, we will look at what an investment plan is, and how you can create one that is custom-fit to you and each of your goals. As we go through the steps below, keep in mind that you may need a few separate written investment plans if you have multiple goals that you're trying to achieve—for example, you may have one investment plan focused on your goal of Financial Freedom, and another focused on paying for your children's college education, or starting a new business.

Step 1: Determine your goal

The first step is the easiest: identifying the specific investment goal you want to achieve. You need to know where you want to go before you can set a practical plan for getting there. So, right now, think about the most important goal you want to achieve—the one that would significantly impact your life. Whether it's working for Financial Freedom, buying a second home, putting a child through college, or something else entirely, clearly defining this goal will help you set a plan designed for reaching it.

Step 2: Determine your time horizon

Once you have identified your goal, you need to determine your investment horizon—i.e., the length of time you plan to hold your investments before you need them to fund your goal. If you have a long investment horizon (think seven to 10 years or more), you may be able to take on more risk in your portfolio because you have more time to ride out any market fluctuations that may come your way. If you have a short investment horizon (say, less than three years), you may want to focus on more stable investments to help protect your capital so that your money is there when you need it.

This ties into the fourth principle we covered in the previous chapter, which taught us that the longer you can stay invested, the greater the chance of having positive returns.

Step 3: Select the target investment allocation

Next, you will need to determine the amount of risk you are willing to take to pursue your goals. By this, I mean the maximum amount of risk to your portfolio that you could sustain before you would need to change your strategy in response to it. This is your "sleep factor"—the amount of downside portfolio risk you can endure without losing sleep.

Your sleep factor is critical when selecting the correct allocation to fit you and your goals, because if you cannot stay invested in your strategy long enough to possibly benefit from compounding returns, then it will be hard to achieve the investment results you want or need. Typically, if you have a low tolerance for portfolio risk, you may want to consider investments that are less volatile, but which may offer a lower rate of return.

Conversely, if you have a higher tolerance for risk, you may be comfortable with more volatile investments that may offer a higher rate of return. It's important to understand, however, that investors seeking higher rates of return should be willing to accept periods of low or even negative returns, possibly lasting for an extended period.

I encourage you to be brutally honest with yourself on this point, because not only will your investment goals depend on it, but also your quality of life. I have seen too many people answer this question the way they *think* they should be invested rather than how they would *prefer* to be invested, based on their sleep factor. It's a critical difference that can have significant consequences, because people who invest the way they *think* they should are, from the beginning, putting themselves into an ill-fitting portfolio that they may panic over and bail out on at the first sign of trouble in the markets. Remember, no matter how aggressive or conservative your plan is, the goal is to stick with it—which means you need to have the confidence that it will help you achieve your goal.

The following chart looks at six different portfolios with varying characteristics. Take a moment and review them, considering the points we have just discussed in this chapter, and then mark the one you feel best fits each goal you seek to complete. You should do this separately for each goal, as the right mix for one may not be right for another.

Investing in the financial markets entails some degree of risk. Investors who seek high rates of return should be willing to accept periods of low or even negative returns, possibly over extended periods of time. The table below demonstrates the trade offs between average return, likelihood of losing money in any one year, and how extreme the declines may be. Review each hypothetical portfolio and select the one that you would be most comfortable with. (Please choose one.)

Portfolio Statistics	☐ Portfolio A	☐ Portfolio B	☐ Portfolio C	☐ Portfolio D	☐ Portfolio E	☐ Portfolio F
Percent in equity	11%	20%	40%	60%	80%	100%
Average return	2.50%	3.25%	4.50%	6.00%	%7.25	8.25%
Maximum decline in portfolio value	-5%	-10%	-22%	-34%	%-44	-53%
Probability of loss in any one year	6%	7%	17%	20%	22%	24%

These statistics are intended to illustrate the variability of returns associated with each type of hypothetical portfolio. Past performance is no guarantee of future results. The maximum decline represents the largest decline in value that the hypothetical portfolio would have experienced. The duration and time period of the decline may be different for each portfolio. The probability of loss represents the percentage of historical returns less than zero that the hypothetical portfolio would have experienced in any one-year period. The hypothetical portfolios do not represent any specific product of performance. More information is available upon request.

Step 4: Assign accounts to each of your financial goals

At this point, you must identify the investment accounts you will assign towards each goal. For some of your accounts, those goals will be straightforward—for example, employer retirement plans, IRAs, and Roth IRAs would very likely be assigned to your retirement goal, and your college savings accounts would be assigned to your educational funding goal. Others may not be quite so clear, or may have multiple designations. For instance, you may have an investment account that you may use to fund the purchase of a second home, but if not used for that purpose would be used for your Financial Freedom goal. In these cases, just do your best to assign a specific goal to each account; you can always go back and adjust them later.

The reason this is such an important step is that different goals require different investment strategies, so you want to be sure that your investment allocation towards that goal is optimal.

Step 5: Evaluate your current investment allocation

Now that you have determined the target investment mix for your goal, you will want to make sure that the current allocation for these accounts matches the target. We'll use the Financial Freedom goals to demonstrate this process.

a. Gather up all your investment account statements and organize them by goal. For your Financial Freedom goal, these assets may include your current employer's retirement plan, traditional IRA, and Roth IRA.

b. Determine the current investment allocation for the total portfolio assigned to this goal. This can be a little tricky to do on your own, so you could work through this step with the help of your advisor or Money Mentor. Alternatively, you could do it on your own with the help of an asset allocation calculator and your most recent investment statements.

c. Once you have completed these steps, you can compare the current investment mix to the target investment mix for this goal.

Step 6: Fit your investment allocation to your goal

The final step in fitting your investment mix to your goal is bringing your current allocation and target allocation into alignment. There are at least two ways that you can do this.

The first is to change the target investment mix to meet the current investment mix on the accounts, which means simply keeping your current investment strategy in place. You would do this if you determine that you are comfortable with your current allocation, and thus there are no further adjustments you need to make.

However, you may want to take the other choice and move your current allocation to fit your target allocation. For example, if you determine that you are invested 10% too heavily in stocks, then you would reduce the stock exposure by that amount to bring it into better alignment.

If you do choose to go with the second option, it is important to note that you should do so with some caution and full awareness of any tax consequences that could be incurred by carrying out this realignment. Your Money Mentor and tax professional could greatly assist you here.

The Benefits of Finding Your Investment Fit

The aim of the process above is to fit your investment portfolio to you and your goals so that you will stay committed to your investment strategy through all the varying market conditions you will face on your journey, both good and bad. I would highly recommend that you repeat this process periodically for each of your goals, so that your investment mix keeps up with you as you work towards achieving them. The case study below is a good illustration of this principle in action.

It was about a year before Sam was planning to retire, and he wanted to confirm that his allocation was where it needed to be on his 401k, which was his primary account for funding his goal of Financial Freedom. The stock market had gone on a tremendous run over the previous few years and had provided him with positive returns, encouraging Sam to become even more stock-oriented in his portfolio. This strong market performance had also created a significant overweight to stock within his portfolio.

Sam was happy with his recent returns, but was growing concerned that he should not be taking so much risk so close to retirement, and was beginning to become concerned about what a market drop might do to his investments. This led him to review his investment mix on his current employer's retirement plan, which was his primary account for funding his Financial Freedom plan. As he worked through the process, he discovered that he was over-allocated to stocks based on his risk profile and his goals for the account. This led Sam to adjust his investment mix with the help of his Money Mentor, which lowered his stock allocation to better fit him and his plan.

In retrospect, this was a good move for Sam, as the market corrected just a few months before his retirement. These adjustments saved him a lot of money and kept him on target for his planned retirement date.

What Level of Confidence Do You Have?

Before we move on to the next chapter, I encourage you to reflect again on your current investment mix across your portfolio. Are you confident that it aligns with you and your goals? If not, I encourage you to come back to this chapter later and walk through these steps again, either by yourself or with the help of your financial advisor or Money Mentor, so you can develop an investment plan and portfolio allocation for each of your primary wealth goals.

Now that you understand how to fit your investment strategy to you and your goals, the next chapter will show you how you can take that strategy through *passive investment cash flow*, which can help you create a portfolio that could last as long as you need it to.

Key Takeaways

The six steps of devising your investment plan are:

- Determine your goal.

- Determine your time horizon.

- Select the target investment allocation.

- Assign accounts to each of your financial goals.

- Evaluate your current investment allocation.

- Fit your investment allocations to each of your goals.

*If you don't find a way to make money while
you sleep, you will work until you die.*

WARREN BUFFETT

CHAPTER 7

FOCUS ON THE FLOW

Paul and Nancy retired in early 2008. They thought they had done everything right: they'd prepared a written wealth plan, had worked hard to complete the action steps required, and thought they were all set to enjoy Financial Freedom. But a severe stock market correction, which cut the value of their retirement assets by over 30% in the first year of their retirement, changed all that. Their feeling of joy and excitement for what they could do in the years ahead—trips, greater freedom to pursue their interests and hobbies, and time with friends and family—was replaced by fear and anxiety.

What made matters even worse was that the stock market stayed down for a year or two, which required them to make some tough choices. As neither of them wanted to return to work, they had to either reduce their lifestyle costs to adjust for their loss in investment value, or begin taking out a greater rate of withdrawal from their investments than they could reasonably support over the long term and hope that the stock market recovered in time.

Like Paul and Nancy, the financial fear that most of us have is running out of money, or having to decrease our lifestyle when we stop working. A passive cash flow stream from your investments that is greater than your lifestyle needs could be the key to reducing both of these fears. As noted author and investor Robert Kiyosaki puts it, "The key to financial freedom and great wealth is a person's ability or skill to convert earned income into passive income and/or portfolio income." While passive income takes a lot of effort to create, once it is established it may provide a recurring stream of cash flow that requires little or no effort to maintain.

But, what exactly *is* passive income, and how can we use it to help you create a more permanent portfolio?

The Benefits of Passive Cash Flow

What passive income means when it comes to your portfolio is income that your investments generate without you having to sell any of them off. This income stream can come in a variety of forms—dividends, interest, rental payments, capital gains, royalties, etc.—and can help lengthen the holding period of your investments, because you may not have to sell any shares to fund your lifestyle.

This is particularly beneficial to investors in the type of down market that Paul and Nancy found themselves in. Extending your holding period prolongs the amount of time your investment strategy can take advantage of potential long-term gains in the market, thus giving you a chance of benefiting from compounding interest year in and year out. This follows investment legend Charlie Munger's maxim that "The first rule of compounding is never to interrupt it unnecessarily."

If you can stay invested regardless of what life, the economy, or the investment markets throw at you, you may not be forced to sell in a bad market. Then, the growth in value of your assets over the long term, in addition to the passive cash flow it provides, could be another potential source of lifestyle funding when market conditions improve.

The ability to not be forced to sell in a bad market is central to the concept of *Sequence of Return Risk*, which is one of the biggest risks that investors face once they reach their goal of Financial Freedom and then need to begin pulling money out of their portfolio to fund their lifestyle. Sequence of Return Risk is the danger that the timing of withdrawals from your investment accounts could damage your overall return by forcing you to withdraw (i.e., sell) your investments in a down market to provide for your income needs. This requires you to sell more shares to maintain your current income level, because the price is low and possibly dropping. If this goes on for too long, especially in the early years of retirement (like for Paul and Nancy), it can put the long-term health of your portfolio at risk, and may increase the likelihood that your portfolio is depleted during your lifetime.

To better understand Sequence of Return Risk, let's consider these hypothetical sequences of returns under two five-year market scenarios. You will notice that the returns are the same, except for their order: Scenario A starts strong and finishes poorly, while Scenario B does just the opposite.

	Scenario A returns	Scenario B returns
Year 1	25%	-20%
Year 2	15%	-5%
Year 3	5%	5%
Year 4	-5%	15%
Year 5	-20%	25%

The table above is for illustrative purposes only and not intended to be reflective of results you can expect to achieve.

This difference in the sequencing has no impact on the investment value if no additional contributions are made, or distributions are taken during this period. In this scenario, a $1 million investment at the end of this five-year period will be $1,147,125 in both scenarios, representing an average return of about 4%.[13] So, investors who are neither putting money in nor taking money out are a little more indifferent to the sequencing of their returns.

However, suppose money is taken out of the portfolio on an annual basis to fund your lifestyle needs, which would be the situation for most investors who have stopped working. In that case, the results will vary in just this brief period.

Let's assume that $50,000 each year is withdrawn to fund lifestyle needs for the five years in the above example. In Scenario A, the portfolio value would be slightly over $933,000 at the end of this period. But, in Scenario B, these same withdrawals would mean that the portfolio would be worth a little less than $816,000—a difference of over $117,000, changing nothing but the order of the returns.

Clearly, the order of returns matters when you are taking money out of your portfolio to fund your lifestyle if you have to sell investment shares to create this income. Another challenge is that you will not know in advance which scenario you will face when you begin taking money out, as you have no control over what type of market you will face in those early years of retirement. But utilizing a passive cash flow strategy may allow you to essentially take luck out of the equation and help protect your Financial Freedom plan from the sometimes destructive effects of Sequence of Return Risk.

So, the next question is: How can you build a passive cash flow for yourself?

Types of Investments

The first step is to familiarize yourself with the various investments that can provide a passive stream of cash flow. Below are some of the most common types that you will come across in your investment portfolio, along with a brief description of each.

a. **Cash or cash equivalents** These are short-term investments that can be easily liquidated, carry low risk of loss, and are designed to preserve capital and earn a small return in the form of interest or dividends. These investments can include savings accounts, money market accounts, certificates of deposit, or certain treasury bills. Cash investments are often considered a low-risk option for investors who wish to prioritize safety over higher returns.

b. **Bonds** Bonds can be issued by corporations and government institutions. Depending on the type you obtain, they can have unique features related to duration (i.e., how long you have to hold on to it before your principal is returned), interest payment, risk level, and return potential. What they all have in common, though, is that in return for your investment into the bond, you will be paid a set amount of interest (often referred to as the "coupon rate") at regular intervals until the bond matures, at which time your principal is returned.

Bonds are designed such that principal and interest payments are all made; however, money can be lost, which is even more so the case for corporate and/or junk bonds.

c. **Stocks** A share of stock represents ownership in a company, while a dividend is a payment made by the company that represents a return of some of the company's profits and/or current earnings to its existing shareholders. These dividends are not guaranteed, and can vary from year to year. The underlying common stock is subject to market and business risks, including insolvency. So, focusing your stock investments on more established companies that are financially sound and have a strong reputation may give you a better opportunity to earn a stable, strong, and possibly growing dividend, and therefore a higher investment cash flow.

d. **Real estate** The passive income generated by your investments in real estate comes in the form of rental payments, which is probably the asset class that first comes to mind when thinking about passive cash flow investing. However, it may not be as truly passive as the others that we have listed so far. When it comes to real estate, you have to find good tenants and keep them happy so that they continue to pay the rent. This requires additional maintenance and repair costs, possible debt service to fund the purchase, and any applicable taxes. So, when looking at potential real estate investments, you should pay attention to the net rental yield a given property can provide after factoring in all these costs. Because of these added complexities, investors often turn to professional managers for help overseeing this asset class.

While these are the most common types of asset classes used to create passive income, there are many other possibilities as well. For example, if you have creative talents, you could write a book or create a piece of art; develop intellectual property, such as a trademark or patent; or even launch an online business. The sky really is the limit when it comes to novel ways for developing passive income, and all it requires from you at the outset is a shift in mindset. Instead of being focused on working to build your wealth and fund your goals, start thinking about how the assets in your Financial Freedom portfolio can start doing some of that work for you.

Taking Action

Of course, while learning more about passive cash flow is important, it is just the beginning of the process for building it for yourself. The next stage is understanding the actions you will need to take to begin building your passive income stream to help fund your Financial Freedom goals. I've outlined the steps below:

a. **Calculate** how much income you need your portfolio to generate for you to meet your Financial Freedom goals. You can refer to your Financial Freedom goal worksheet from Chapter 3, or use your current income as an estimate.

b. **Determine** the current level of passive income your portfolio generates for you. Once you have this amount, you can work to determine your *income yield*—that is, your income-only return on investment, which is calculated by taking your dividends and interest payments and dividing them by the value of the investment, expressed as an annual percentage. You can then take this income yield and estimate your passive cash flow for when you want to achieve your Financial Freedom goals by multiplying it by your portfolio value at that time. You now have an idea of how much passive cash flow could be available to fund your lifestyle.

c. **Compare** the level of passive cash flow you will have at retirement to what you will need it to be to achieve your Financial Freedom goals by subtracting the value in a) from that of b).

If the result of that final calculation tells you that you're right on target or have more than you need to fund your Financial Freedom goal, great job! If not, don't be discouraged—there are three useful ways to help close that gap.

i. First, you can tighten up your budget and reduce your income needs to fit the level of passive cash flow you want at the time of your Financial Freedom goal. Start by identifying anything in your budget that could be reduced or eliminated without being too big of a sacrifice to your overall quality of life, and cut them. This can make achieving your goal much more possible.

ii. Next, you can increase your annual contributions between now and when you want to retire so that your investment portfolio can work to generate your desired level of passive cash flow at your current income yield. To begin this process, you could utilize the freed-up cash flow you created in the step above.

iii. Lastly, you could further diversify your portfolio into more income-producing assets that may allow you to increase the yield on your portfolio without increasing your contribution rate. This higher yield could provide the passive cash flow needed to fund your Financial Freedom at that time.

The bottom line is that when the amount of passive cash in your portfolio is greater than your lifestyle expenses, you have created a portfolio that may be sustainable for as long as you need it. Knowing if your portfolio can handle the market's ups and downs without possibly impacting your lifestyle can give one a good feeling, so you don't have to share the misfortune Paul and Nancy experienced at the beginning of the chapter.

However, I do have some good news to report about them. With a slight adjustment to their portfolio allocation to put more emphasis on the cash flow it provided to them, and a little tightening of their budget, they could create a more suitable scenario without having to return to work. And you can work to have a similar situation without the stress by simply beginning to think of your assets not only in terms of the overall return provided, but also the income.

As we conclude this chapter, we will examine an additional benefit that an adequate level of passive cash may provide: greater investment flexibility.

The Impact of Passive Cash Flow

Mark and Rita were disciplined investors, having stayed the course with their portfolio strategy through the many ups and downs the market had thrown at them over the years. They enjoyed being more growth-oriented and preferred maintaining a larger amount of stock in their portfolio, because they believed stocks were the best place to grow their assets.

This strategy had worked well for them, and they had accumulated enough to achieve their Financial Freedom goal. Still, they came to see me because they were wondering about the best way for them to start creating income from their investment portfolio once they retired without dramatically altering their allocation towards stocks.

The answer was to find a way for their portfolio to generate enough passive cash flow each year through dividends and capital gain distributions to fund their needed income. So, following our conversation, we began to carefully shift more of their assets to dividend-paying stocks, being mindful of the potential tax consequences of any changes we made.

This new approach helped fund their lifestyle needs, while maintaining a growth focus that they felt worked best for them. They had their necessary income and did not have to be overly concerned with the fluctuations in the market, because they did not have to sell any of their investments to create their income. In fact, this strategy allowed them to actually benefit during market downturns, as they could add to their stock holdings when they were down in value.

This chapter concludes the section of the book focused on investment strategies and the principles you can use to help fund your goals. We will now shift our attention to some advanced planning concepts that are designed to help you maintain your Financial Freedom once you have reached it.

Key Takeaways

- Understand the benefits of passive cash flow.

- Shift your mindset to focus more on investment cash flow in your portfolio.

- Know how much of it you will need to reach your Financial Freedom goals.

- Start working towards increasing it within your investment portfolio.

PART 3

WORKING TOWARDS SUSTAINING FINANCIAL FREEDOM FOR THE LONG HAUL

You must pay taxes. But there's no law that says you gotta leave a tip.
MORGAN STANLEY

CHAPTER 8

REDUCING TAX DRAG ON YOUR PORTFOLIO

Josh and Lori came to see me a few years ago. He was an engineer, she was a teacher, and they both believed in the importance of saving for their future. They worked hard and made smart financial decisions as they pursued their dream of retirement, including maxing out what they could invest each year in their employer retirement plans, which came with a match on part of their contribution. This helped them lower their current taxes, as their contributions and earnings would only be taxed once they pulled them out when they retired. While this was a nice benefit, they began to think this may force them to pay more taxes later, and so they wanted to evaluate their other options.

The conversation I had with them highlighted the importance of creating a tax-diversified investment strategy that is designed to reduce the overall tax drag on your portfolio over the life of your accounts—which means the reduction in the total return of your portfolio due to taxes. Reducing this impact on your portfolio can make a difference to the success of your plan. And it doesn't take much of a difference in your portfolio returns to have an impact, as the example below will demonstrate.

Let's compare the results of two different one-time investments of $500,000 over a 10-year period to see how a small difference in returns can have a big impact on results. One investment averaged a 6% return, allowing it to grow to approximately $895,000 over this timeframe. Another investment was able to generate a 7.5% return, allowing it to grow to approximately $1,030,500. As you can see, even a slight improvement in your return can impact the end results.

Simply put, working to reduce the tax drag on your investment portfolio could help you achieve your Financial Freedom goals more quickly. So, let's start learning about the types of taxes that can impact your portfolio returns.

Types of Taxes

To begin with, you need to "know your enemy." Two types of taxes that can have a big impact on your portfolio are ordinary income tax and capital gains tax.

Ordinary income tax is paid on any earnings your investment portfolio creates, like dividends and interest. It is also the tax rate you pay on any withdrawals from retirement accounts such as IRAs, employer plans, and on any working income. Ordinary income tax rates are generally the highest tax rate most investors pay.

Capital gains tax is paid on income generated from the sale or exchange of an asset within your portfolio that is worth more than your original investment. It is important to note that there are two types of capital gains: short-term and long-term.

Short-term capital gains are realized from the sale of assets held for one year or less, and are typically taxed at the same rate as your ordinary income. By contrast, *long-term capital gains* are realized on the sale of assets held for more than one year, and typically receive the more favorable capital gains rate. So, when evaluating your portfolio, it is important to pay attention to how long you have owned the asset.

Since different types of taxes will apply to your portfolio, you will want to limit taxes that may have the biggest impact on your wealth as you grow and distribute your accounts and strive to promote the most tax favorable ones. This process is known as *tax diversification*, which entails placing your investment assets in different types of accounts that are taxed differently and are designed to provide greater tax efficiency for your whole portfolio. So, it is very much an issue of having the right types of assets in the right accounts at the right time.

The primary account types at your disposal for this process are:

i. *Taxable accounts*, such as bank and brokerage accounts

ii. *Tax-deferred accounts*, such as IRAs and 401ks

iii. *Tax-exempt accounts*, such as Roth IRAs and municipal bonds

Having assets in each of these accounts works to give you the flexibility you need during the withdrawal stage to help reduce your taxes. This is important for your Financial Freedom, because tax rates may increase with a growing national deficit in the United States. But, just as investment diversification helps to mitigate exposure to any single asset or risk, tax diversification may allow you to structure withdrawals in retirement to potentially increase the amount of after-tax spendable income. By doing this, it could help you reduce the risks of fluctuating tax rates, and work to keep more money in your pocket.

The bottom line regarding tax diversification is that, with proper planning and the right tax allocation strategy for your portfolio, you can work to reduce which taxes you must pay during the accumulation and, later, the distribution of the assets. Remember, it is not how much you earn, but how much you *keep* that can determine the success of your Financial Freedom plan over the long haul.

So, with that in mind, let's go over a few practical ways you can set up tax efficiency of your portfolio, both now and in the future.

Step 1: Strategically position your accounts for tax efficiency

The first step is to review your portfolio to evaluate what types of assets are held within each account type. This is because simply changing the *placement* of your assets, and not your assets or investment approach, may provide you with additional returns.

If possible, you want to match up your most tax-efficient assets (i.e., those that do not generate much taxable income or gains) into your taxable accounts, and the most tax-inefficient assets (those that do generate a substantial amount of taxable income or gains) into your tax-deferred or tax-exempt accounts. For example, municipal bond investments and growth stocks could be held more efficiently in a taxable account, for they typically distribute little or no taxable income each year. Taxable bond investments, higher dividend-paying stocks, and more actively traded accounts, which typically create more capital gains each year, could be held more efficiently in a tax-favored account such as an IRA or Roth IRA.

To begin with, inventory your current investment accounts to review your asset locations. Make a detailed list of your accounts by type (taxable, tax-deferred, or tax-exempt), along with their respective values. For example, your employer plans (like 401k and 403b) and traditional IRAs would be considered tax-deferred accounts; your standard investment and bank accounts would be taxable accounts; and your Roth IRAs would be tax-exempt accounts.

Step 2: Identify and correct inefficiencies

The next step is to identify the type of investments in each account to see if any inefficiencies can be corrected. Examples of these inefficiencies could be having taxable bonds in a taxable account, when a tax-free bond would make better sense; or, having your highest income-producing assets in a taxable account, when a tax-deferred account may work better. Determining where these potential inefficiencies exist will require a thorough analysis of your portfolio, with the help of your advisor or Money Mentor.

If you do discover any tax inefficiencies, you can start evaluating the adjustments you need to make to your portfolio to reduce the tax drag on your returns. However, make sure you do this with the help of your tax advisor, so that those adjustments can be made with as little tax impact as possible.

Step 3: Evaluate investment management styles

Further on the point above, you will also want to evaluate your investment management style within your different accounts. An active investment style may better fit tax-deferred or tax-advantaged accounts, while a more passive investment style could work better in a taxable account.

Let's take a closer look at each of these styles. Before we start, though, let me stress that the definitions below are just that—definitions, not a judgment on which performs better or worse. For the moment, the purpose is to show how each management style impacts tax drag.

i. An *active investment approach* requires ongoing management of what positions to hold, buy, or sell at any given time. Its goal is to outperform the market based on knowledge and selection.

A good example would be an actively managed mutual fund, where a professional manager or team of managers oversees this process on behalf of investors who have pooled their dollars into this fund. In their efforts, they more frequently buy and sell positions within their portfolio (known as *portfolio turnover*) to try and take advantage of market trends or inefficiencies.

This kind of trading activity can lead to a higher tax drag for investors, making it less tax-efficient than passive investing, as the turnover creates more taxable activity. This is why this investment approach may work best in a tax-deferred or tax-advantaged account, where this activity can be better sheltered.

ii. A *passive investment approach*, as the name suggests, requires less action on the part of a manager once the portfolio is established. An example of this would be an index fund that seeks to replicate the performance of a given index. Here, the manager initially selects investments that they feel would achieve this objective and then makes little to no changes over time. This helps decrease portfolio turnover, which can help limit the tax drag on the portfolio and can have the effect of lowering operating fees. Therefore, this investment style may work best in a taxable account.

Again, my goal with the above is not to convince you which approach is better for your portfolio; that's a conversation you should have with your Money Mentor or financial advisor. Rather, I simply want to educate you on the tax impact of each investment style on your portfolio returns.

Tax diversification may also help when you begin withdrawing dollars from your portfolio to fund your Financial Freedom lifestyle. The example below illustrates how this could work in the distribution stage.

Susan, who is 62, just retired and needs to begin withdrawing money from her portfolio. Her portfolio consists of a traditional IRA worth $750,000, a Roth IRA worth $250,000, and a brokerage account worth $500,000. Her goal is to withdraw $50,000 from her accounts this year with as minimal a tax impact as possible.

So, she sat down with her advisors, who outlined the following options for her needs for the year:

- She could pay ordinary income taxes at a rate of 20% on any distribution from her traditional IRA, which would equate to $10,000 ($50,000 at 20%). This would net her $40,000 to use as income.

- She could pay capital gains taxes of approximately $6,000 to withdraw the $50,000 from her taxable investment account. This would net her $44,000 to use as income.

- She could pay no taxes to withdraw the $50,000 from her Roth IRA, as she has had this account for over five years and is over 59.5 years old. This would leave her the full $50,000 to use as income.

After considering these options, Susan decided to pull her current year's distribution from her Roth IRA to minimize the tax impact in the current year. She was happy that she had this flexibility, and plans to have the same conversation with her advisors next year to decide her best course of action, because what works in one year may not be what works in the next.

Step 4: Tactics for tax-efficient investing

The final step to consider relates solely to your taxable accounts, such as brokerage accounts. In these accounts, you can harvest any capital losses your portfolio has experienced to help offset current and future gains. This is done by selling investment positions currently trading at a loss.

A *capital loss* occurs when you sell a position in your portfolio for less than what you invested. For example, if you invested $100,000 and it is now worth $80,000, then you can sell this position and take a $20,000 capital loss on it. This loss can offset any gains made in that same year, and, if there happen to be more losses than gains in the current year, then you can carry these losses into future tax years to help off-set future gains or income.

However, it is important to note that there may be limitations on how much you can deduct in any one given year. This strategy can be implemented during market corrections while positions are down, allowing you to effectively take a negative (such as a market correction) and attempt to make it a positive by reducing tax drag by taking capital losses.

It is important to note that there will be many factors for you to consider in determining whether this option is right for you. But, if you have taxable investment accounts, I encourage you to sit down with your tax professional, in conjunction with your financial advisor or Money Mentor, and perform a detailed analysis of your tax situation and portfolio to see if this, or any of the other ideas in the chapter above, would be right for you. This analysis may result in discovering capital losses that could be harvested, or a more tax-efficient way of owning your investment accounts.

This type of collaborative review can be a valuable tool to help you work towards reducing the tax drag on your portfolio by identifying the right tactics for you and your situation. Then, your team can help you implement these tactics in an efficient way. It would also provide the benefit of a more thorough knowledge of your own tax situation than you had before, which is the first step in having a better understanding of your taxes.

Last but certainly not least is the benefit of simply having your tax professional and your Money Mentor on the same page concerning your tax situation. This way the decisions you make on your portfolio can be balanced, with the perspectives on taxes and on investment markets both impacting your decisions with neither one necessarily being favored, nor either being excluded from the conversation.

The Benefits of Tax Diversification

Given the current tax environment we find ourselves in, taxes are one of the most significant expenses or drags on your portfolio returns. Creating a more diversified portfolio by having the right investments in the right accounts can help save you money, and potentially promote more robust after-tax returns. It may also give you the flexibility and control you need during both the accumulation and distribution phases of your investment life, which could allow you and your family to maximize the benefits of your wealth. As the renowned British economist John Maynard Keynes put it, "The avoidance of taxes is the only intellectual pursuit that carries any reward."

Developing a strategy to create a tax-efficient investment could be at the foundation of your comprehensive wealth management plan. However, with the state of change in the tax code, investment markets, and the types and number of investments available to investors, you should strive to develop a dynamic plan that is managed by a trusted team of experts. That's what Josh and Lori were able to take advantage of after we sat down to go over their portfolio in detail.

To address their concerns about having their retirement savings in one type of account, Josh and Lori decided to split the contributions in their employer plans into two buckets instead of just one. Part of their contributions continued to be invested in the traditional 401k plan, which helped lower their current taxes because these contributions were not taxable to them in the year they were made. The other part of their contributions was put towards a Roth 401k plan that was available to them, which did not help them reduce their current taxes, but gave them the potential for tax-free withdrawals in the future. Through this strategy, they were able to lower taxes now, and achieve greater tax flexibility in the future.

The next step in our advanced planning process is to discuss protecting the cash flow and wealth you have created, so that you may avoid unnecessary planning setbacks that could delay the achievement of your goals.

Key Takeaways

- Understand the impact of tax drag on your plan.

- Consider the ideas presented in this chapter for helping to reduce tax drag on your portfolio.

    a. Understand the tax diversification of your portfolio.

    b. Utilize the proper asset location to possibly achieve better tax efficiency now and in the future.

    c. Determine the proper alignment of investment management style and account type.

    d. Harvest capital losses on your portfolio to offset gains.

- Review your tax situation and portfolio collaboratively with your tax professional and Money Mentor.

*Unprecedented events occur with some
regularity, so be prepared.*

SETH KLARMAN

CHAPTER 9

PROTECTING YOUR WEALTH AND CASH FLOW

n 2013, the life insurance gap for Generation Xers was almost $450,000, which marked an increase of 24% over the five-year period prior.[14] To put that in perspective, think about what this gap would mean to your family's future if it applied to you. That amount could pay off your mortgage and give you greater stability. It could pay for college tuition for your kids, setting them up for a great start in life. Or it could be invested and used by your family to provide a stream of income in your absence. Regardless of how you would use this amount, it would clearly be a big help.

I understand that insurance is not a particularly fun topic to discuss, as it requires us to think about all the bad things that could happen to us. However, it's critical to have that discussion, because I've seen the results of this insurance gap and what it means to a family's future and their ability to reach their wealth goals. I want to help you understand that your family doesn't have to experience that kind of misfortune.

This chapter will show you how you can avoid potential insurance coverage shortfall by understanding the major risks to your financial future; evaluating your current insurance gaps, if they exist; and taking a critical action step to fill this gap. Before we begin, though, I want to take a minute so we can consider the primary benefits of having the right coverage to protect the wealth you've worked so hard to build.

The Benefits of Wealth Protection

The first benefit is simply knowing that if any ugly situation happens to you, like premature death or disability, your family will be okay. It can also help that, should any of these events occur, your basic financial needs will be provided for (a *huge* benefit), and your wealth goals for those you love can potentially stay on track. This way, you can know that your family's future is on a firm foundation.

Having the right protection can also help you maintain your progress towards your important goals, like your goal of achieving Financial Freedom. Imagine that you've worked hard on your Financial Freedom fund over the years, and it has grown to the point that you can now really feel confident that you'll be able to hit your objective. Suddenly, a loss, an accident, or another unfortunate event occurs that puts these funds at risk due to inadequate coverage. If this loss were to occur, you may have to start from square one and rethink your goal; at the very least, your goal of Financial Freedom would be delayed. However, with proper coverage in place, you can help keep your Financial Freedom journey on track.

The knowledge that you have done a thorough review of your coverage, and determined that it is adequate to meet your needs, can free up the energy that you may otherwise have spent worrying about the what-ifs and let you channel it towards more productive things, like your relationships, growing your career, or simply enjoying life. A much better way to spend your mental focus than worrying, if you ask me!

With all that said, let's have this un-fun conversation now so that you can devote more time and energy to your most cherished goals, and the many other positives in your life.

Medical Insurance

One of the most basic risks to address is the costs of medical care related to sickness or injury, whether now or in the future. It will come as no surprise that these costs can add up quickly, and can significantly disrupt your wealth plan if you're not properly insured. Recent data shows that the average hospital stay costs about $13,000, while many of the most common surgeries run into the tens of thousands—not to mention the costs of regular doctor visits and/or prescriptions.[15]

Proper coverage can help limit out-of-pocket payments for medical expenses such as these, even if it won't eliminate them. These costs, including your premiums, can still feel like a substantial amount—indeed, in some cases they can come to several thousand dollars per year—but could be much less than the total cost of care you would incur without coverage. This highlights the main concept behind insurance coverage: using a small portion of your wealth each year to help protect a much larger amount.

This type of coverage is often provided through your employer plan as a benefit, and can have many moving parts. For this reason, I would highly encourage you to pull out your benefits summary, review what you have, and reach out to your benefits team with any questions. If you are self-employed, or retired and not yet eligible for Medicare, you will need to obtain private insurance coverage. For additional help in determining which coverage is right for your situation, you could reach out to a health insurance consultant for advice on which plans provide you with the best fit, taking into consideration your specific needs and medical history.

Life Insurance

Another risk that can potentially put your family's finances at risk is the death of a primary wage earner.

This is particularly impactful in the early years of wealth development, when your wealth base is smaller.

This risk can be covered through life insurance, which comes in many shapes and sizes. There are too many to cover in detail in this chapter, but it's important to understand at least the two basic types of policies: term life insurance, and whole life insurance.

Term life insurance covers you for a fixed period—typically 10, 20, or 30 years—and, if you die within this time frame, the insurance company will pay out the stated death benefits. These premiums, along with the death benefit, typically stay level throughout the term of coverage. It is generally considered the most economical way to obtain the coverage you need, particularly during the early years of your wealth journey.

For term life insurance, the length of the term should ideally match the risk you are trying to cover. So, if one of your concerns is to be able to fund your children's college education, then your term needs to last until your youngest child would be projected to complete college.

Whole life insurance is a form of permanent coverage, with benefits lasting for your lifetime. Because its benefits extend for a longer period, the premiums are generally higher than for the same level of term insurance, because there is an increased likelihood the insurance company will have to pay out benefits. There is also a build-up of the cash value that accumulates within the policy, so whole life plans also offer a savings element to them. But, like term coverage, the premiums and death benefits are usually level through the policy's life.

Determining the right type of coverage for you, then, depends on both your coverage goal, and how much you can comfortably budget towards it without sacrificing too much of the cash flow that may be needed to help fund your other goals. However, I believe the more important question is: *How much insurance do you need to have to protect your loved ones?*

Again, like many other financial questions we have addressed in this book, there is not one standard answer that works for everyone. So, let's see how you can go about putting a number to that.

Step 1: Determine your insurance "needs"

a. First, ask yourself this question: "What do I *need* my insurance to cover?"

As we've said above, this is very subjective, and will vary from person to person and family to family. However, some common items in the "need" category include paying off mortgages, college loans, paying for end-of-life expenses, or covering a certain number of years' worth of income. Whatever you determine your most vital needs are, write them down, along with their approximate value; if you like, you can use the worksheet provided at the end of the chapter.

Step 2: Add your insurance "wants"

b. Now, ask yourself: "What do I *want* my insurance to cover?"

Here, you will likely want to list your most important financial goals, such as your Financial Freedom goal, any charitable giving you would like to do, providing for your children in terms of education or other considerations, etc. Add these "wants" to the worksheet, along with their approximate value.

Now, add the total costs of your "needs" and "wants" together. This will provide you with an estimate of the level of coverage you will want to consider.

(Before we move on to the final step below, you should ask yourself one more very important question: *If you or your partner were to die right now, would the survivor be able to stay on track with your most important wealth goals and take care of the family?* If the answer is yes, then you can move to the next step; if the answer is no, then I would advise you to re-evaluate both your "needs" and your "wants" until you arrive at coverage that would account for that possibility.)

Step 3: Review your balance-sheet assets

c. Now, with your coverage estimate completed, you should review the assets on your balance sheet to determine how much you have there that could help provide for these funding targets upon your passing. These would include items such as savings, investment accounts, and the retirement accounts that you have accumulated to this point.

Step 4: Calculate your insurance requirements

d. Once you have totaled these accounts, the last step is to subtract the value of these assets from the amount of coverage you estimated in the previous section. This is the amount of the gap in your life insurance coverage.

I apologize for all the math in this section! To help make it a little easier for you, I have provided a worksheet at the end of this chapter to walk you through each of the steps above. To help you further with understanding this process, let's look at the case study below.

Bill and Mary needed life insurance on each of them to cover five years' worth of income and enough to pay off their mortgage, which was their only debt. These two items amounted to $1,250,000. They also wanted it to cover the costs of putting their two kids through college, which they estimated at $250,000.

They had already saved about $50,000 for college expenses, and had another $50,000 set aside in an emergency fund. However, they did not want to factor in any of their investment or retirement accounts into this decision, so they excluded them. This left them with a target amount of $1.4 million of life insurance coverage needed for each of them.[16] They then compared this number to their current amount of coverage, and realized that they each had a $400,000 gap in coverage that they needed to address.

Disability Income Coverage

Moving to another area of risk, one that is more likely to occur than costs stemming from premature death is loss of income due to disability.[17] This is an issue that sometimes does not get the attention it deserves, which means that it's even more important that you give it some serious thought.

To begin with, ask yourself the following question: "What would be the impact on my financial condition if I was unable to work due to a prolonged sickness or disability?" Adding that time element to this question is key. My guess is that most of the readers of this book could handle a short-term loss of income due to ill health by dipping into savings or investments. However, the impact that an extended illness or disability could have upon your income could be catastrophic. To illustrate this, consider the following scenario.

Imagine that you are 15 years away from your planned retirement date, and, although you appear to be on target, you need to accelerate your savings in the coming years to get where you want to be in terms of portfolio value. You also have three children you will be helping through school and getting started in life during this same time.

Suddenly, the unexpected happens: you are involved in a significant auto accident, causing you to suffer injuries that mean that you will not be able to return to work for a considerable period. Complicating the situation further is that you don't have adequate disability income coverage in place.

Without that coverage, you may be forced to begin drawing money out of your investments and savings to help provide for your family while you recover. This may work in the short run, but every day you do so it puts you at a potential greater risk of running out of funds later in life—because not only do you have to withdraw those funds before you planned to, but you are also less likely to be able to contribute anything to them to make up for what you've withdrawn.

That's a real double whammy to your wealth accumulation and goal achievement. This is why protecting against this potential loss of income is so important. By doing so, you leverage your wealth through the payment of premiums, and transfer at least some of this risk to the insurance company.

Personal Liability Coverage

The final risk I want to address in this chapter is something that can also be missed in your planning. This is the *personal liability risk* you may encounter beyond what your current coverages (like home and auto insurance) may account for. The type of insurance that addresses this risk is referred to as *umbrella insurance*, because, like an umbrella, it covers liability beyond what your other coverages can handle, meaning that you do not have to cover that liability through your assets or cash flow.

To illustrate this, let's return to the example above where I asked you to imagine the impact of a loss of income due to a disability resulting from a car accident. Let's further assume that you were at fault for this accident and have been sued by the other people involved, resulting in a judgment against you of $2.5 million. The situation just went from bad to worse, right?

Without umbrella coverage, you would be liable for any amount over what your auto insurance policy covers. Let's say your home and auto policies combine to provide for $750,000 of liability coverage. This would mean that you have to make up the difference of $1.75 million by either liquidating your assets—meaning that they're not available to help you deal with your personal loss of income due to your disability—or, worse, filing for bankruptcy, if you don't have enough assets to cover the damages. Either way, this would deplete your wealth and your ability to reach your most important financial goals on schedule.

Fortunately, umbrella coverage can remove the possibility of this nightmare scenario, and the cost of this coverage is generally relatively small compared to the potential impact of possibly not having it. So, hopefully, the question you're asking yourself now is not, "Do I need umbrella coverage?" but rather, "How *much* umbrella coverage may I need?"

To properly evaluate this, I suggest that you review your balance sheet again and see if you have at least enough coverage to protect your current level of assets. This way, if you are sued (as in the scenario above), none of your personal assets would be at risk. But also, keep in mind that your assets, if properly managed, will grow over time, so you may have to add coverage in the future.

Wealth Protection Review

The various risks and coverages we've addressed above are just some examples of what you need to consider to protect your wealth and avoid possible setbacks to your wealth plan. The most important takeaway from this chapter is that you do a full review of your coverage with your financial advisor or Money Mentor, in tandem with an insurance specialist(s), to see if you have adequate protection to fit your plan.

Once you provide them with a summary of all the current coverages that you have in place (including your personal lines of insurance, like home and auto coverage), they can help you evaluate it and determine whether any changes need to be made based on the coverage you have and the goals you are trying to accomplish. It may be the case that, even if you are properly covered or have more coverage than required, they may find some cost savings that could be used elsewhere in your plan, which could help you progress towards your most important financial goals more quickly.

A word of caution here: be alert to the possibility that you may have *too much* coverage, and are thus "insurance rich." You also don't want to have too much of your cash flow tied up in insurance policies rather than investments, which may grow at a better rate if you devoted more resources to them. Consider the example below.

A few years ago, Nick and Sarah sat down and reviewed their coverage with an insurance specialist, following the recommendation of their Money Mentor. They thought they were in pretty good shape and had done all they needed to protect their wealth against the various risks they may face, but they wanted a detailed review as they got nearer and nearer to their goal of Financial Freedom.

What they discovered surprised them: they had nearly twice the coverage they needed, particularly in life insurance. This was because a) they obtained this coverage about 25 years ago, when their children were still in their home, whereas now they were all out of college and starting their own lives; and b) Nick and Sarah had accumulated enough wealth that the risks they needed covered were one of them to pass away had significantly diminished.

This discovery led them to reduce some of their coverage with the help of their insurance specialist, which reduced their annual premium outlay and allowed them to contribute more to their invest-ment savings. They felt it was a double win for them, knowing that they had the proper amount of coverage to protect their wealth while increasing what they could set aside for their Financial Freedom fund.

The intent of this chapter was not to go "into the weeds" on every kind and every aspect of insurance policies available to you. Rather, I wanted to give you a big-picture view of the basic elements you need to begin putting together the wealth protection plan that works best for you, and make sure that the amount of coverage you have is intentional and directed towards advancing your wealth goals.

Now that you have ideas to help properly protect your assets and cash flow, the next step is to evaluate your estate plan so that you could leave a legacy for your family, loved ones, and others you want to benefit.

Key Takeaways

- Understand the risks to your wealth plan and cash flow, and commit to finding the proper insurance coverage to protect them.

- Evaluate your current coverage to see if it fits your plan.

- Consider the benefits of a full insurance review of your coverage to determine which areas are lacking, and/or areas where you have too *much* insurance.

*A good person leaves an inheritance
for their children's children.*

PROVERBS 13:22 NIV

CHAPTER 10

LEAVING (AND RECEIVING) A LEGACY

Music icon Prince sold over 100 million albums over the course of his four-decade career, allowing him to build a net worth of over $250 million by the time of his premature death in 2016 at the age of 57. After his passing, however, it was discovered that he had died without doing any estate planning—not even a will, that most fundamental document that directs who is to receive the benefits of your estate.

Because Prince had died without leaving a will, it came down to a judge in his home state of Minnesota to direct the dissemination of the artist's wealth based on state probate rules. This left Prince's family in limbo and incurred many legal fees before the affair was ultimately settled after many years.

While there was surely never *anybody* like Prince, when it comes to estate planning, his was not an isolated case. According to a 2023 study, over 70% of

Americans do not have a documented estate plan.[18] However, there are ways to reduce the kind of problems that Prince's heirs encountered by undertaking some of the basic estate planning that we outline in these steps, which are designed for you to leave your legacy to the people and places you care about the most in a direct and efficient manner. By reviewing these steps, they may help *you* decide where your hard-earned wealth goes in the end, not a judge in a courtroom.

Before we get started, though, it's important to note that legacy planning has two poles: first, the leaving of a legacy; and second, the *receiving* of that legacy, which requires an equal degree of preparation. You will need to have a plan in place for both of these in creating your legacy, whether it's one that you're building, or one that you're inheriting from your parents or family members. Therefore, we'll begin this chapter with some practical tips for leaving your legacy, and conclude with some best practices for inheriting one.

But first, we need to answer a key question: What exactly *is* your legacy?

Defining Your Legacy

Most people think of their legacy solely in terms of the assets that they own upon their death. While this is indeed a large part of one's legacy, there's another part that doesn't involve money. Your legacy is also the values that helped you build your wealth in the first place and that you want to promote after you leave. A sound legacy plan will encompass both elements and give you the chance of making a lasting, positive impact on your loved ones for generations to come.

So, before we get down to the nuts and bolts of legacy planning, let's first consider those values that allowed you to build a legacy in the first place. Think of this as your *wealth story*—the better you understand it and communicate it to the next generation, the greater the chance your legacy plan may succeed.

Here are a few questions that can help you start writing your own wealth story:

i. What is the most valuable thing that your wealth provides to you?

ii. What is/are the most important principle(s) that helped you manage your wealth successfully?

iii. What is the biggest mistake you made with your wealth, and that you would want others to avoid?

iv. What do you want your wealth to do for others after you're gone?

v. What *don't* you want your wealth to do for others after you're gone?

Take some time with your answers, and be completely honest with yourself. If you have a partner, I encourage you to complete this exercise together to ensure you're on the same page.

Communicate Your Legacy Plan

The next step is to communicate your wealth story to your beneficiaries, so that they know and appreciate the values and principles that drove it. A legacy without a narrative can be received by its inheritors as simply a jackpot to be squandered away; conversely, properly communicating your wealth story may possibly be your best opportunity to create generational wealth.

To help accomplish this, consider taking some or all of the following actions:

i. Create sound legacy planning documents with an attorney that clearly communicate your wishes for your wealth.

ii. Explain to your beneficiaries your wishes for how you would want them to use their inheritance wisely now. Based on the answers to the questions listed earlier in the chapter, this can be done through direct conversations, a letter, or even a video.

iii. Hold a family meeting or retreat to convey your intentions in a more "formal" manner. Your Money Mentor could facilitate this discussion.

iv. Give your beneficiaries a small portion of their inheritance during your lifetime and evaluate how they handle it. This provides an opportunity to coach or correct them if either is needed.

Questions to Consider for Your Estate Plan

The next step is to review the balance sheet you created in Chapter 3, which represents the wealth portion of your legacy. Once you've fully re-familiarized yourself with it, it's time to consider the fundamental questions below, which will drive your legacy planning.

i. Who do you want to manage the distribution of your assets to your beneficiaries?

This individual would be the executor of your will, and be responsible for ensuring your wishes are followed and how your assets are managed in the meantime. It could be a family member, friend, trusted advisor, or even an institution, such as a trust company. Whoever you choose, though, it must be someone you have a high level of confidence in, and faith in their ability to follow the instructions you've laid out for them in your estate plan. It's important to note here that your executor has no personal discretion in distributing your wealth: they will be charged with following through on your wishes.

ii. Who do you want to benefit from your wealth after you're gone?

For most of us, this will include our children and/or grandchildren. It may also be an organization, such as a church, non-profit, or alma mater, or some combination of several parties or groups.

iii. When and how do you want your beneficiaries to receive your wealth?

This is a critical question if you have beneficiaries who, due to age or ability, would not be able to wisely steward a large amount of money if they received it all at once. A potential solution here is to provide these beneficiaries with limited access to their portion of your wealth until they reach a certain age (or indefinitely, depending on the situation), with the oversight of a trustee. This is one of the advantages of proper legacy planning: you can extend your control of your wealth beyond your lifetime to give your loved ones the chance of success in how they make use of it.

iv. If you have minor children, who will take on the responsibility of raising them after your death?

I know this is a hard thing to think about for those in this situation, but it may also be the most important question to answer. The person you decide on may be the same person in charge of managing your estate assets, but it doesn't have to be if you want to keep these roles separate. This separation of roles would allow the guardian to focus on raising the children, and the trustee to focus on the management and distribution of the assets. This may be the right course of action for you if the person you have named as guardian is not the best to manage the trust assets, or vice versa. However, if you do separate these two roles, you will want to evaluate their ability to work together for the benefit of your children.

Estate Planning Documents

With the fundamental questions above addressed, it's time to look at the basic planning documents you will need to execute your plan. These are:

i. a will,

ii. a revocable living trust, and

iii. power of attorney documents.

Please note the below is only a high-level overview of these documents; a more detailed application will be made with your estate planning attorney or specialist.

i) Will

As we noted above, a will is a basic legal document that allows you to control the distribution of your assets after your death. It specifies who should inherit your assets, how much they should receive, and when they should receive them; the party responsible for managing this distribution and paying off any outstanding debts (i.e., the executor); and the person who will assume the role of guardian if you have minor children.

Without a will, the distribution of your assets will be determined by the laws of your state, which may not align with your wishes. This is why a will is a fundamental building block of most estate plans.

Something to note here is that your will is a public document. This means that any items distributed through your will to your beneficiaries are part of the public record, and can be viewed by anyone after your death. So, if privacy is necessary for you, you will want to consider looking at other distribution methods for your estate.

Another important aspect to flag here is that any of the assets that pass through your will must go through a process called *probate* before they reach your beneficiaries. In this process, a state court reviews the deceased person's assets, determines the beneficiaries, and verifies the will is valid before the assets are distributed. The rules that govern this process vary from state to state, and it will frequently incur additional costs against the estate, in terms of both fees and the time it takes to complete the process, which can often run into months.

These are some of the reasons why it is common practice to avoid probate where possible. One way to do this is through a revocable living trust.

ii) Revocable living trust

A revocable living trust is a legal arrangement established during your lifetime to protect your assets and then distribute them upon your death. It is like a will in this regard, but there are a few key differences worth noting.

One of the ways a revocable living trust differs from a will is that it is typically more expensive to set up initially due to its more comprehensive nature, as it deals with issues pertaining to you while you are still alive as well as after you pass away. However, when you consider the long-term benefits of avoiding the probate process, a living trust can often be more cost-effective.

A trust also can hold and manage assets after your death, which can come in handy if you want to spread out the receipt of assets over time instead of all at once to help prevent your legacy from hurting rather than helping your beneficiaries. Similarly, if you have minor children, a trust can allow the necessary time for them to grow up and mature, to the point where they can steward their inheritance on their own.

An important note here is that once you have completed a revocable living trust, you also must transfer assets into it for it to take effect. Unfortunately, many people have gone to the trouble and cost of creating a trust and then failed to put assets into it. Without taking this step, a trust will be of little value to you, because the trust can only control the property that is placed into it.

So, if you do go to the trouble and expense of establishing a trust, you will want to retitle your investment and bank accounts into it. You would also want to retitle any other property, such as your home, rental property, or other business assets into it as well. Key members of your Financial Dream Team could be most helpful with this step.

A frequent question I get from my clients is, "Which is best suited for my situation: a will, or a trust?" While I always advise you to seek the guidance of an estate planning attorney who can consider the specifics of your situation, there are a few basic questions you can ask yourself that may help you determine which is right for you. If the answer to any of the questions below is yes, you may want to consider a revocable living trust:

a. Do you want the content of your estate to remain private upon your death?

b. Is your net worth over $1 million?

c. Do you own property in multiple states?

d. Do you want your beneficiaries to have quicker access to your assets?

e. Is the potential for estate taxes a concern for you?

Generally, the best candidates for a revocable living trust are those who prioritize privacy, have a larger net worth, and want to pass their assets on to the next generation while avoiding probate. However, it's also important to note that there are other ways than a revocable living trust to avoid probate on your assets. One of them is to name *account beneficiaries.*

Most investment accounts, allow you to name account beneficiaries in a beneficiary list. This can be a critical document, as it supersedes your will or trust in directing the assets after your death. And importantly, just like assets that pass to beneficiaries through a trust, any assets that pass through a beneficiary listing also avoid the probate process.

This is why it's important to review and update these beneficiary listings regularly to ensure they stay current with your wishes. For many, this can be a very efficient and economical way to transfer your assets while avoiding probate. I want to share a story with you to help put this into perspective.

Troy started contributing to an IRA before getting married, and named his two siblings as equal beneficiaries of the account upon his death. A few years later, he married Erica, and they went on to have two children. Troy continued to contribute to his IRA over the years, and the value grew to well over \$100,000.

Sadly, Troy passed away in his early forties. When Erica tried to access the value of his IRA, she discovered that Troy had never updated the beneficiary listing to include her and their children. This made a very difficult time even harder, as Erica had to work with Troy's siblings to access the funds.

This unfortunate situation could have been avoided if the beneficiary listing had been updated—a simple, no-cost step that requires only signing a form with the IRA custodian. This is why it's important to ensure that the beneficiary listings for your accounts are up to date, and to review them periodically to ensure they stay current.

iii) Power of attorney

Power of attorney documents round out your estate plan. They address not what happens to your assets upon your death, but who manages your assets and your health care if you cannot do so yourself while you are still alive. There are two types of these documents: one for your property, and the other for your health care decisions.

A **durable power of attorney for property** allows you to name a person (a power of attorney, or POA) who can make financial decisions for you if you become sick or incapacitated. When this power is active, your POA can act as if they were you. Having this document in place can save the time and cost of naming a POA after you need it, with the help of the courts.

A **durable power of attorney for health care** allows you to name a POA who can make medical decisions for you if or when you cannot do so yourself. They can also make end-of-life decisions for you with the help of doctors, based on the wishes you outline in this document.

Clearly, you need to have high trust in the people who you designate as POAs. The people you name in these positions will have power over both your money and your life, so, obviously, you will want to take great care in selecting them. In many instances, spouses are often each other's POA, with a child as a backup if required. However, your POA does not have to be a family member: it could also be a trusted friend, or a professional who is qualified to carry out your wishes.

Postscript: How to create your estate planning documents

Before we move on to the concluding section of this chapter, a brief word is in order about how you should go about creating your estate planning documents. There are a couple of primary ways you can go about this.

The first method is to use an online platform. This is certainly a cheaper option, and can be effective, but the documents you produce through this method may not fit exactly what you are trying to achieve. They may also have a greater risk of being contested, which could create problems (and costs) for you and/or your estate.

For these reasons, I encourage you to consult an attorney who specializes in estate planning to help you create your documents. While this will cost more than a tool you find on the internet, it could save you a lot of hassle in the long run. If you decide against this, however, you should at the very least review the online documents that you have created to be certain they are in good order.

Receiving an Inheritance

Up to this point in the chapter, we have focused on how to *leave* a legacy for others. Now, it's time to learn about how to *receive* a legacy wisely. This is even more important now, because the wealth that will likely transfer in the next few decades as the baby-boom generation passes away could be in the tens of trillions of dollars.[19] And obviously, if you are one of those on the receiving end of this wealth transfer, you could potentially accelerate your own Financial Freedom goals by how you manage it.

Before we move on, a word of caution. Even though an inheritance may be of tremendous help in pursuing your goals, you don't want to have to *rely* on it to do so. You can't be certain whether you will receive such a legacy, or, even if you do, it may be less than you expected.

With that proviso out of the way, let's look at a few best practices for inheriting a legacy wisely.

Take it slow (but beware of deadlines)

One of the most important things you can do when receiving a legacy is to take it slow. You don't have to make any immediate decisions about how you should manage the assets you inherit. This can be a very emotional time, as you may be dealing with losing a loved one, so giving yourself some space to heal before you make any major financial decisions can be a huge help when it comes to optimizing these assets. They will be there when you're ready to deal with them.

However, I will add one caveat to the above: you do need to be aware of certain IRS guidelines relating to the timing of distributions. A good example is if you inherit retirement accounts such as a traditional IRA or Roth IRA, as penalties may apply if distributions are not taken out on time. You will also want to know any tax filing deadlines for income or estate taxes.

That said, at this time, you should focus on your family first and only turn to the financial side when you're ready.

Utilize your Financial Dream Team

When you've determined that you are ready to deal with your inheritance, it's important to engage the counsel of your Financial Dream Team. You'll need them, as there are so many facets to receiving an inheritance—from the distribution of the assets, to how they are taxed, to how they can be best invested and used to promote your success.

So, when you're ready to begin making decisions on your inheritance, reach out to your Money Mentor, financial advisor, attorney, and tax specialist to help you optimize these assets. This group is not there to tell you what to do, but to help you understand the advantages and consequences of each potential decision so that you can make the right decision for your own situation. Remember: they work for *you*, not the other way around.

Using your inheritance

There are a few main ways to use your inheritance. You can a) spend it, b) invest it, c) bless others with it by giving it away, or d) do some combination of all three.

The key to optimizing the legacy you receive is determining which portion of it you will allocate to each category, so that they can have a long-term benefit for you and your family. This allocation will be different for everyone. For some, the right thing will be to pay off some debt (e.g., a mortgage). For others, it may mean giving away a portion of their inheritance to continue their family legacy of generosity. Others may want to invest most of it towards their Financial Freedom fund. And, yes, some will want to spend it on something they've always dreamed of.

All of these can be worthy choices, so long as they fit within the plan and legacy of the inheritance. So, as you evaluate the best thing to do, you should ask yourself two important questions:

Will this decision help me with my most important financial goals?

And, equally importantly:

Does my decision honor the legacy and values that were used to create this wealth in the first place?

Another critical aspect to consider here is all the various tax consequences involved in inheriting assets—for they are many, ranging from ordinary income tax to capital gains tax. In some cases, this may also involve estate and inheritance taxes, which can be applied at both the federal and state levels. These can be significant. As of 2024, the federal estate tax rate starts at 40% for estates that exceed $13,610,000 (this is double for married couples).[20] Additionally, many states also have their own estate tax rules that must be factored in. So, while these taxes don't apply in many cases, when they do it can be very painful.

This is where the counsel of your Financial Dream Team can be invaluable, because the tax impact on an inheritance can get really complicated, really quickly. So, before making any decisions, make sure you're aware of the tax consequences. Remember: the more you can keep, the more you can do for yourself and others.

Putting It All Together

As we noted above, everyone will have their own particular rationale for allocating legacies they receive. That said, the case study below offers an excellent example of how one of my clients distributed their inheritance in a way that had a positive impact on themselves, their children, and many others outside their family circle.

Lori had just received a large inheritance from her family's estate. Fortunately, her parents had completed their estate plan and kept it up to date regarding the changing tax laws, the estate's growth over the decades, and what they wanted that legacy to do for their family after they were gone. They wanted their legacy to be a blessing for their children and grand-children, and, as they had fully communicated their wishes both within their estate planning documents and to their family directly, they had done all they could to ensure this would happen.

Knowing how much work had gone into not only creating this wealth, but also planning how it would be distributed, Lori wanted to ensure she did every-thing she could to steward it wisely. This was her state of mind as she and her husband John met with me to discuss their best course of action. They told me how Lori's parents had built this wealth through their entre-preneurial spirit, hard work, and generosity, and that they wanted to honor this legacy by handling their inheritance within the framework of their own wealth plan.

To begin with, they decided to use a portion of the inheritance to help their children with college costs, and to get started in life with a down payment on their first home. They also added a portion of it to their Financial Freedom funds. But—and this is the unique part of this story—Lori and Josh also committed to giv-ing much of that legacy away over the course of their lives to organizations that were doing great work in their community. It was a wonderful blend of honor-ing the legacy of Lori's parents, along with achieving some of their personal wealth goals.

Finally, there was another crucial part of this leg-acy that Lori and John inherited. Now that they had experienced to the full all the work that Lori's parents had put in to develop their estate plan, and seen how much benefit it was to them in the distribution of their estate, they committed to updating their own estate planning documents to make sure that they could someday pass on their own legacy to their family in the same way.

Estate planning is an essential step in ensuring that the legacy you leave behind reflects your values and intentions, benefiting your loved ones and avoiding unnecessary complications. As illustrated by the case of Prince, failing to plan can lead to prolonged legal battles and uncertainty for your heirs. By taking proactive steps to create a comprehensive estate plan, you can safeguard your wealth, support your family's future, and preserve the principles that guided your financial success.

Whether through wills, trusts, or other legal instruments, a well-thought-out legacy plan can provide clarity while allowing you to leave an enduring positive impact on the people and causes you care about most. As you embark on this journey, remember to communicate your wishes clearly, involve your beneficiaries, and seek professional advice to navigate the complexities of estate planning effectively.

Key Takeaways

- Recognize that the legacy you leave encompasses more than your monetary wealth; it includes the values that shaped your wealth-building journey.

- Communicate with and mentor your beneficiaries to ensure they manage their inheritance wisely.

- Identify and select the key players in your legacy plan.

- Prepare the essential planning documents for your legacy plan: a will, a revocable living trust, and power of attorney for both property and health care.

- Engage an estate planning attorney to draft your legacy plan.

- Adopt best practices for managing and inheriting wealth responsibly.

When performance is measured, performance improves. When performance is measured and reported back, the rate of improvement accelerates.

PEARSON'S LAW

CHAPTER 11

TRACKING AND UPDATING YOUR PLAN

en and Katie had always diligently saved for retirement. They'd done the planning work, knew what they needed to do to reach their Financial Freedom goal, and believed they were on their way to achieving it. Most of their debt had been paid down, and they had both been maxing out their contributions to their employer retirement plans for several years.

However, as they were talking over dinner one evening, they realized that they hadn't updated their plan since they first created it. Suddenly, a wave of anxiety washed over them, as they realized they were not actually certain if they were on track to achieve their goals.

Fortunately, once they gathered and reviewed the statements for all their retirement accounts, they were pleasantly surprised to find that they were ahead of schedule. Understandably, this gave them a deep sense of relief, but also of motivation. Having that certainty made them feel more confident about where they were in relation to their target, and inspired them to keep working hard to achieve it.

Ben and Katie's story highlights the benefits of tracking your Financial Freedom goals. Setting goals and creating your plan is an important part of the planning process, but without proper tracking it can be challenging to stay motivated and focused on taking the required and sustained actions that are necessary. When you track your goals, you create a system that helps you measure your progress and provides you with the feedback you need to keep going in the right direction and at the right pace. This will be the topic that we address in this final chapter.

However, before going over the what and the how of financial plan tracking, let's briefly discuss how tracking your goals can serve as a valuable motivational tool.

Tracking Your Progress

To track your goals is to hold yourself accountable for your actions. Tracking reaffirms your commitment to working towards your Financial Freedom goals in a certain timeframe, and spurs you to take the actions needed to potentially accomplish them. This dynamic is especially heightened when you work with a third party—i.e., your Money Mentor or financial advisor—to help you do it. I often hear from my clients that they had taken a certain action step, like increasing their contribution rate or talking to an attorney about updating their will, because they knew I would be asking them about it at our next visit.

In addition to encouraging you to take necessary actions, tracking also allows you to course-correct when you see that a particular action or strategy isn't working. And, if you track your progress regularly rather than at long intervals, it allows you to make minor, easier adjustments along the way instead of having to make major pivots at a later stage. One example of this that I see regularly in my practice is annual contributions to an employer retirement plan. Checking your progress at least once a year based on your current contribution rate allows you to see if you're behind pace, and thus need to increase your contributions to get back on track.

Furthermore, tracking can provide you with confidence, as it allows you to focus on the progress you've made instead of the gap that remains between you and your goal. Also, it can shift your perspective from the obstacles in your path to the possible solutions for them. Dan Sullivan, in his book *The Gap and the Gain*, highlights the impact this can have, stating: "your future growth and progress are now based in your understanding of the difference between the two ways in which you can measure yourself: against an ideal, which puts you in what I call 'the GAP,' and against your starting point, which puts you in 'the GAIN,' appreciating all that you've accomplished."

So, while striving to reach your goal, do not forget how far you have come on your wealth journey. This can help keep you motivated and moving forward towards your goals.

Updating Your Plan

Before we get down to the nuts and bolts of tracking your financial plan—which begins with identifying the most important items to track, and then breaking down each of these into smaller components—I would like to address a common question regarding reviewing a financial plan: namely, How often should you review it?

I've said it before, and now I'll say it again: as always, there is no one universally applicable answer to this question, as everyone's situation is different and unique. That said, I advise my clients that their plan should be reviewed at least once a year, to allow for the kind of minor course corrections we described above. For example, it will be much easier to increase your contribution rate to your employer retirement plan from 12% to 15% if you discover you're off pace, rather than hiking it from 5% to 15%.

However, tracking your progress once a year is not always enough—there are times when you should review it more frequently. The first of these is when you are nearing one of your primary goals, as you don't want to discover any nasty surprises. Another reason for more frequent reviews is when a major change happens in your life, like a death, divorce, a transition to a new job, or a sale of a business, as events such as these can impact your plan. This is why one of the first questions I ask each time I meet with a client is, "What has changed personally, professionally, or financially in your life since we last met?"

It can also be important to have more frequent conversations about your plan when there is a lot of market volatility, causing a lot of fluctuations in your investment values. This can be an unnerving time, and many people can naturally worry that it will get them off track. So, it never hurts to refresh yourself with the current state of your plan in such situations, even though you may find that your plan is still on target despite the volatility in the market.

Ultimately, the frequency of review is up to you. So, you need to ask yourself: How often do you want to dive back into the details of your plan? The answer will differ for everyone. Some of my clients like to review quarterly, while for others it can be challenging to get them to review annually. My commitment to them is to meet with them at the pace that works best for them. If you are working with an advisor, you will want to communicate your preferred pace so that you can be on the same page with them from the beginning of your relationship.

Advanced Planning Review Steps

When you review your plan, you will want to address the advanced planning categories we have looked at throughout the book, and your overall investment strategy. Just before we dig in, I want to offer you this word of encouragement: the review process doesn't have to be complicated to be effective. What I've seen to be very effective with my clients is to focus on one to two items in each of the areas that need to be addressed. After you've gone through those, you check them off and move on to the next. It can be that simple.

The advanced planning section of your plan comprises the three main areas covered in the book: maximizing your cash flow, taking care of your heirs through legacy planning, and protecting your wealth against the risks that could set you and your goals back. Let's go through each of them in turn.

a. **Tracking your cash flow.** By either increasing cash flow into your household through additional revenue, or decreasing the flow out of the household, you may increase what is known as the *financial margin* that you have available to help fund your goals. So, a good measure of the progress you are making in your plan is to evaluate this financial margin to see which direction it's heading in. This metric can be determined by updating your budget or cash flow report, which I suggest doing quarterly. If it's increasing, great; if it's not, then you should try to determine why this is the case, and what needs to be done to correct that trend.

A great way to potentially free up additional margin is a thorough review of your tax situation to see if there's anything you can do to put more money in your pocket and less in the government's. You can look at your recent tax returns to see if any opportunities exist within your portfolio or income structure to effect this. A useful metric to track here is your average tax rate, which is usually summarized on your return. Again, remember that it doesn't take a lot of change in your situation to make a difference: any money you manage to free up can now start growing inside your investment strategy to help fund your goals or improve your lifestyle.

b. **Tracking your legacy planning.** To begin with, if you haven't drafted these documents with the help of an estate planning attorney, that should be first on your list. Once that's been done, make sure to do a quick review of the documents to ensure they correctly indicate the people you've appointed as beneficiaries, successor trustee of your trust, executor of your will, agents on your power of attorney documents, and, if you have minor children, the guardian you named to take care of them. This is a very basic step, but an essential one, particularly if any changes in your family or life situation necessitate that you change any of the parties appointed to these roles.

c. **Tracking your insurance coverage.** As we've covered previously in this book, your needs change over time, and you need to make sure that your insurance coverage keeps up with your situation. Tracking the effects of those changes could reveal that you need to add more coverage, or, conversely, that you now have too much coverage and so can scale back.

As with your legacy plan tracking, another aspect of this review will be to check the beneficiaries listed on your policies to ensure their accuracy. Your Money Mentor and insurance specialist can be tremendously helpful in this process.

Tracking Your Investment Strategy

Once the three advanced planning categories above have been addressed, the next step is to review your investment strategy for each of your most important goals.

First, you will need to refer to the goals sheets that you completed in the earlier exercise (see Chapter 7) to see if the asset allocation strategy you are using for each goal still fits you and your plan. This is because as you approach one of those goals (like Financial Freedom), you may need to revise your allocation as you move from the accumulation stage to the distribution stage. Also, the economic and market backdrop is always changing, which may present you with a good reason or opportunity to tactically shift your approach. So, to complete your review, walk through the steps of the Chapter 7 exercise once again to see if you need or want to make any adjustments.

Next, you will want to evaluate your performance to see if it is appropriate for the given level of risk you are taking. This can be done by comparing the portfolio returns for each of your goals to a benchmark index that most closely resembles the target portfolio you are using to reach your goal. You will also want to evaluate each of your investment holdings or managers against their peers to decide if any changes are merited.

Last, but certainly not least, is to evaluate your portfolio to see if it is as tax efficient as it needs to be, and that you're getting the desired value for any fees you are paying to manage your investment assets. This can be done as part of the tax review outlined in Chapter 9, which I suggest that you do at least annually.

Finding Your Financial Freedom Score

The final stage in the review process is to wrap all these pieces up into one metric, which represents the progress you are making on your goal. Regarding your Financial Freedom goal, you can use a retirement planning calculator to discover the probability score of reaching your target. This score I refer to as your Financial Freedom Score.

To help get an accurate score from this tool, you should typically input such information as a) your investment values, b) the money you are saving each year towards this goal, c) your time horizon, d) your investment allocation, e) your Social Security benefit and pension estimates, and f) a close approximation of how much income you will need to fund your Financial Freedom lifestyle.

Based on this information, the calculator will generate a score that you can use to gauge the strength of your plan. If that score comes back lower than you expected the first time you run this calculation, don't be too discouraged. Rather, take note of it and plan out the steps you need to take to get it on target. For example, if your first score was a 70, and you need to reach at least 90 within the next 10 years, then focus on improving the score by at least two points every year.

Some steps you can take to raise your score could include increasing your contributions, cutting back on your lifestyle needs, or improving your investment strategy—all of which are things that you can control. Then, at your next review, run that calculation again, and be encouraged by the progress you've made in the past year rather than focusing on the gap you still have left to close.

Don't Set It and Forget It

You need a plan that you monitor and update to help you reach your goals. As this next story illustrates, the consequences of not taking these steps can be discouraging.

Chris worked as an engineer for over 30 years, and saved a decent amount of money annually. He had sat down with a financial planner and put together a plan for reaching his retirement goals many years ago, but never bothered to look at it again or keep it up to date. He believed everything would work out if he kept putting money into his plan. But, as he got closer to his target retirement date, he realized that he had no idea how much money he needed to retire comfortably.

At this point he realized he needed to revisit his plan to see if he was on track, but was nervous about what he would find out. Chris wanted to retire in a year, and he was unsure if the numbers would support it. With this mindset, he sat back down with the financial planner to update his plan.

Unfortunately, his fears proved correct. After consulting with the planner, Chris realized that he had not saved enough money to maintain his standard of living if he were to retire in a year. He was told that he either had to reduce his lifestyle to retire at his target date, or that he would need to continue to work for a few more years to build up his retirement funds. Chris regretted not taking retirement planning seriously, and wished he had paid more attention to it earlier in life.

You can work to avoid this by taking the steps now to build your plan and then working to keep it updated as your life and situation change while you journey towards your goal.

Key Takeaways

- Keep your plan updated regularly, as creating it is just the first step.

- Focus on the progress you're making, not the gap you need to close.

- Track the key metrics vital to your success.

- Follow best practices for reviewing and updating your plan.

- Use a retirement planning calculator to evaluate the strength of your Financial Freedom plan.

*Decide where you are going and
how you are to get there. Then make a
start from where you now stand.*

NAPOLEON HILL

CONCLUSION

ongratulations! You've made it to the end of the book, and now have a plan of attack to Win at Wealth and strive for your Financial Freedom. But this ending is a beginning as well: it's your commitment to doing the work that needs to be done to bring your plan to life.

Even now, you may be feeling intimidated about undertaking this journey. Believe me, I understand— the road always looks longest as we prepare to set out on it. But I'd like to share with you the results of a recent study by the Canadian Foundation for Financial Planning, an organization that is dedicated to improving the lives of Canadians by supporting widespread access to the benefits of financial planning.[21] The study found that those with a comprehensive wealth plan in place:

- Feel like they're more on track with their financial goals and retirement plans.

- Are more confident that they can deal with financial challenges in life.

- Are better able to indulge in their discretionary spending goals.

- Have improved their ability to save in the last five years.

These are the kinds of feelings I want you to experience, by having a plan that strives to help you gain and sustain your own unique idea of Financial Freedom. And, in this book, I've outlined the major steps you need to build that plan:

- **Envision** what Financial Freedom really means to you, and use that vision to drive your progress towards that goal.

- **Design** a financial plan and investment strategy based on that vision, drawing on principles that can help you navigate the uncertainty of the investment markets that you will face on your journey.

- **Sustain** the progress you make through such actions as reducing the tax drag on your portfolio, protecting your wealth and cash flow through proper insurance coverage, and planning how to both leave and receive a legacy (inheritance) in a way that means the most to you.

- **Track and update** your plan regularly with the help of your Financial Dream Team, adjusting and course-correcting as your life situation changes while you get closer and closer to your goal.

Remember, having a clear vision of Financial Freedom, and a financial plan, are both essential, but neither will matter unless you take the proper actions to implement them. The Financial Freedom lifestyle that you've wanted—the one where *you* choose how you spend your days, weeks, and years, without having to work and with confidence in your future—is there for the taking, but you need to step up to seize it.

So, I want to ask a favor of you, right now. In the spaces below, write down three initial steps that you've found in this book that could help you begin making progress on your Financial Freedom goals.

Then, circle one of them—preferably the easiest—and commit to acting on it within the next 24 to 48 hours so that you can prove to yourself that you're already beginning to create some positive momentum on your Financial Freedom journey.

1. _____

2. _____

3. _____

Trust me—you've got this!

APPENDIX:
RESOURCES

DREAM TEAM
CONTACT INFORMATION

NAME	ROLE	EMAIL	PHONE
	Money Mentor		
	Financial Advisor		
	Tax Specialist		
	Estate Attorney		
	Insurance Specialist		
	Realtor		
	Lending Specialist		
	Executive Compensation Specialist		
	Charitable Giving Advisor		
	Business Valuation Specialist		
	Other:		
	Other:		
	Other:		

NOTES: _____

_____

_____

_____

_____

BALANCE SHEET

Date: [   ]

ASSETS	GOAL		LIABILITIES	
Cash equivalents			**Lifestyle Debt**	
Checking	Reserve Fund		Revolving Debt	
Savings	Reserve Fund		Other	
Money Market	Reserve Fund		Other	
Total			**Total Lifestyle Debt**	
Investments			**Other Loans**	
Work Retirement Plan	Financial Freedom		Mortgage Loan	
Traditional IRA	Financial Freedom		Home Equity Loan	
Roth IRA	Financial Freedom		Auto Loan / Lease	
College Savings	College		Student Loan	
Investment Account	Goal 1		Business Loan	
Investment Account	Goal 2		Other	
Investment Account	Goal 3		Other	
Total Investments			**Total Other Loans**	
Property				
Home	Property			
Rental	Property			
Other	Property			
Total Property				
Auto				
Vehicle 1	Auto			
Vehicle 2	Auto			
Other	Auto			
Total Auto				
Other				
Business Asset	Financial Freedom			
Other	Other			
Other	Other			
Other	Other			
Total Other				
Total Assets			**Total Liabilities**	
	Total Net Worth			

GOAL GAP WORKSHEET

I would like to _____

by _____

so that I can_____

GOAL FUNDING TARGET

$

LESS

CURRENT GOAL

$

EQUALS

GOAL FUNDING GAP

$

NEXT STEPS

○ _____

○ _____

○ _____

FINANCIAL FREEDOM GOAL / WORKSHEET GAP

(1.) Financial Freedom Cash Flow Target $_____ /MN

Financial Freedom Income Sources

Pensions (if any)	$_____ /MN
Social Security estimate	$_____ /MN
Rental Income	$_____ /MN
Business Income	$_____ /MN
Other Passive Income	$_____ /MN
Other Income Sources	$_____ /MN

(2.) Total Financial Freedom Income Sources $_____ /MN

(3.) Monthly Financial Freedom Portfolio Income Need *(Line 1- Line 2)* $_____ /MN

(4.) Annual Financial Freedom Portfolio Income Need *(Line 3 x 12)* $_____ /YR

(5.) Financial Freedom Portfolio Target Value *(Line 4 x 25)* $_____

(6.) Financial Freedom Portfolio Current Value $_____

(7.) Financial Freedom Portfolio Gap *(Line 5 - Line 6)* $_____

LIFE INSURANCE
COVERAGE WORKSHEET

NEEDS
(EXAMPLES)

Debt Repayment
Final Expenses
Income Replacements

+

WANTS
(EXAMPLES)

Retirement Funding
College Funding
Legacy Gift

-

**LIQUID
ASSETS**

Total Liquid
Assets

=

Funding
Gap

ONE PAGE FINANCIAL FREEDOM ACTION PLAN

Financial Freedom Goals

1. _____
2. _____
3. _____
4. _____
5. _____

Current Planning Tasks

1. _____
2. _____
3. _____
4. _____
5. _____

Current Financial State

Net Worth	$_____
Financial Margin (YR)	$_____
Cash Reserves	$_____
Investment Assets (Total)	$_____
Retirement Assets	$_____
Savings Rate	_____%
Goal 2 Assets	$_____
Savings Rate	_____%
Goal 3 Assets	$_____
Savings Rate	_____%

Investment Planning Tasks

1. _____
2. _____
3. _____
4. _____
5. _____

Task Planning Tasks

1. _____
2. _____
3. _____
4. _____
5. _____

Financial Freedom Score

Financial Freedom Income Need (Per Month)	$_____
Social Security Income	$_____
Pension Income	$_____
Working Income	$_____
Rental Income	$_____
Other Passive Income	$_____
Other Income	$_____
① Needed Portfolio Income	$_____
② Projected Portfolio Income	$_____
Percent of Portfolio Income Funded (2÷1)	_____%

Estate/Legacy Planning Tasks

1. _____
2. _____
3. _____
4. _____
5. _____

Wealth Protection Tasks

1. _____
2. _____
3. _____
4. _____
5. _____

FINANCIAL FREEDOM
ACTION PLAN
ANNUAL REVIEW

Top 3 Wealth Goals I Achieved This <u>Past Year</u>	Top 3 Goals I Want to Achieve In the <u>Coming Year</u>
1. _____	1. _____
2. _____	2. _____
3. _____	3. _____

Financial Metrics Progress	Financial Metrics Progress

	START	END	CHANGE		START	END	CHANGE
Net Worth				Net Worth			
Cash Reserves				Cash Reserves			
Financial Margin				Financial Margin			
Freedom Assets				Freedom Assets			
Goal 1 Assets				Goal 1 Assets			
Goal 2 Assets				Goal 2 Assets			

Financial Freedom Score %_____	**Financial Freedom Score** %_____

Other Goals I Achieved This Past Year	Other Goals For This Year
1. _____	1. _____
2. _____	2. _____
3. _____	3. _____

Next Important Action Steps	Notes
1. _____	_____
2. _____	_____
3. _____	_____

NOTES: _____
_____
_____
_____
_____
_____
_____
_____
_____
_____
_____
_____
_____
_____
_____
_____
_____
_____
_____
_____
_____
_____
_____
_____
_____
_____
_____
_____
_____
_____
_____
_____
_____
_____
_____
_____
_____
_____
_____

FINANCIAL FREEDOM FRAMEWORK

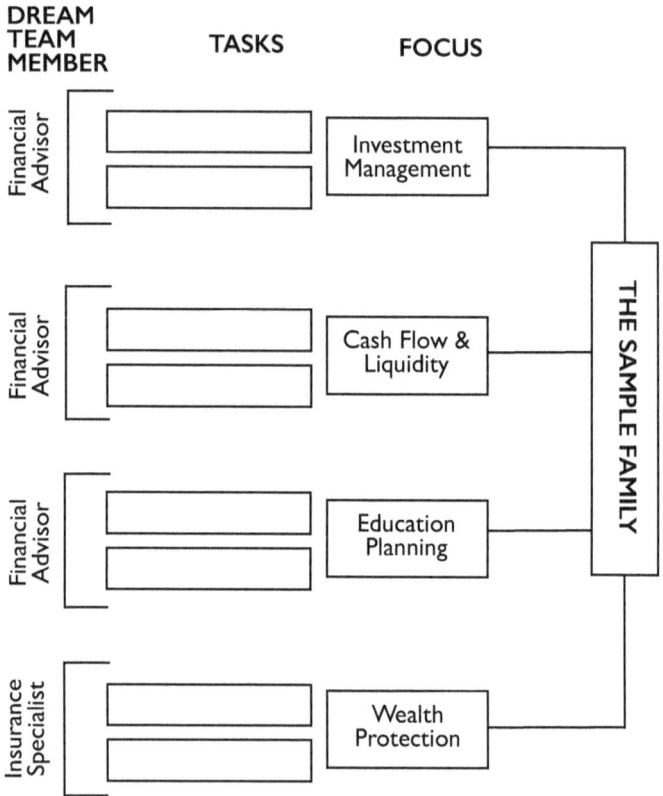

DREAM TEAM MEMBER	TASKS	FOCUS	
Financial Advisor		Investment Management	
Financial Advisor		Cash Flow & Liquidity	THE SAMPLE FAMILY
Financial Advisor		Education Planning	
Insurance Specialist		Wealth Protection	

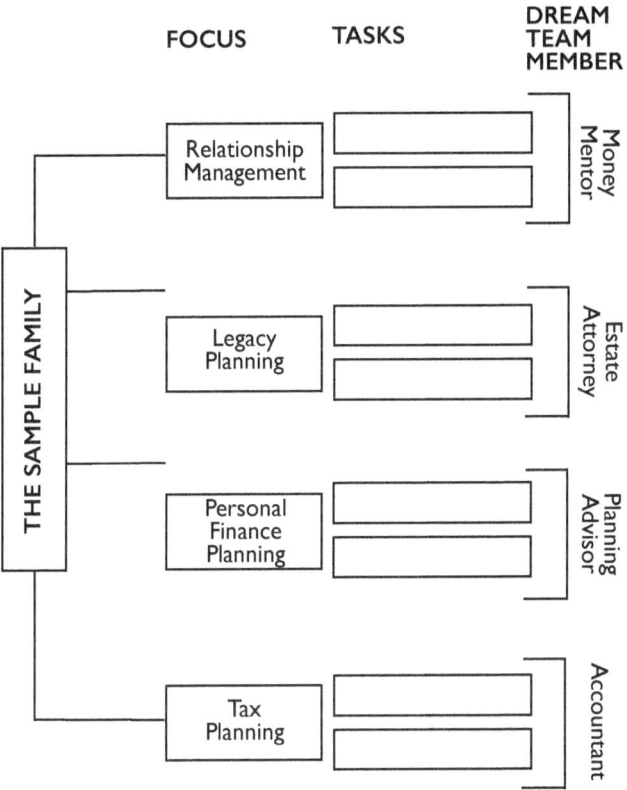

FOCUS **TASKS** **DREAM TEAM MEMBER**

THE SAMPLE FAMILY

Relationship Management — Money Mentor

Legacy Planning — Estate Attorney

Personal Finance Planning — Planning Advisor

Tax Planning — Accountant

CONNECT WITH ME

Thank you for reading *Win at Wealth*. I hope it was a great step towards Financial Freedom and your most important goals.

You should now have a written plan to help guide your next steps on this journey. However, you may still have questions about how to apply some of these ideas, or perhaps you're interested in a personal consultation with me to discuss your situation. If so, I am here to help.

If you would like to learn more about me and my practice and how it can help you Win at Wealth, please visit *www.sjohnson.bairdwealth.com/winatwealth*. Here, you will learn more about my Win at Wealth consultation and how to schedule one with me.

You can also connect with me through:

Email:
sjohnson@rwbaird.com

Website:
www.sjohnson.bairdwealth.com

LinkedIn:
www.linkedin.com/in/scott-johnson-win-at-wealth

I wish you all the best as you strive to Win at Wealth!

ENDNOTES

1   "Most Americans Don't Have a Financial Plan, and Many Think Their Wealth Doesn't Deserve One." 2018. *Businesswire.com*. May 15, 2018. https://www.businesswire.com/news/home /20180515005598/en/Most-Americans-Don%E2%80%99t-Have-a-Financial-Plan-and-Many-Think-Their-Wealth-Doesn%E2%80%99t-Deserve-One.

2   McMahon, Tim. 2014. "US Inflation Long Term Average." *Inflationdata.com*. April 2014. https://inflationdata.com/Inflation/ Inflation_Rate/Long_Term_Inflation.asp.

3   Z, Georgiev, Georgi. n.d. "Time Value of Money Calculator - Calculate TVM." *gigacalculator.com*. https://www.gigacalculator. com/calculators/time-value-of-money-calculator.php.

4   Net annual spending income X (1-tax rate), or $135,000 X (1-0.20) = $168,750

5   Gross annual income/portfolio withdrawal rate = your Financial Freedom value, or, $103,750 / 3% = $3.46 million

6   "Table 15. Life Expectancy at Birth, at Age 65, and at Age 75, by Sex, Race, and Hispanic Origin: United States, Selected Years 1900-2016." n.d. https://www.cdc.gov/nchs/data/hus/ 2017/015.pdf.

7   "Table 15. Life Expectancy at Birth, at Age 65, and at Age 75, by Sex, Race, and Hispanic Origin: United States, Selected Years 1900-2016." n.d. https://www.cdc.gov/nchs/data/hus/ 2017/015.pdf.

8   "Trustees Report Summary." 2019. *ssa.gov*. 2019. https://www. ssa.gov/OACT/TRSUM/index.html.

9   Full Social Security benefits (100%) less projected benefits in 2034 (77%) equals a 23% discount rate.

10 Annual Social Security benefits estimate divided by the proposed withdrawal rate. So, ($2,500 per month X 12 months) / 4% equals $750,000.

11 Kerr, Emma, and Sara Wood. 2023. Review of A Look at 20 Years of Tuition Costs at National Universities. *US News and World Report*. September 22, 2023. https://www.usnews.com/ education/best-colleges/paying-for-college/articles/see-20-years-of-tuition-growth-at-national-universities.

12 "What Past Stock Market Declines Can Teach Us." n.d. *CapitalGroup NACG*. Accessed July 26, 2024. https://www. capitalgroup.com/individual/planning/market-fluctuations/ past-market-declines.html.

13 The average is found by adding the returns of each year and then dividing by the number of years: (25%+15%+5%-5%-20%)/5 = 4%.

14 "Generation X Reveals Dramatic Effects of Great Recession: A Widening Gap in Life Insurance Protection; Shortfall Rises 24% since 2008 according to Unique Comparison Surveys." 2013. *Businesswire.com*. September 12, 2013. https:// www.businesswire.com/news/home/20130912006023/en/ Generation-X-Reveals-Dramatic-Effects-of-Great-Recession-a-Widening-Gap-in-Life-Insurance-Protection-Shortfall-Rises-24-since-2008-According-to-Unique-Comparison-Surveys.

15 Milliken, Maureen. 2018. "Hospital and Surgery Costs—Paying for Medical Treatment." *Debt.org*. 2018. https://www.debt.org/ medical/hospital-surgery-costs/.

16 ($1,250,000 + $250,000) − ($50,000 + $50,000) = $1,400,000

17 "Death vs. Disability – Which Is More Likely?" 2019. *affordableinsuranceprotection.com*. 2019. https://www. affordableinsuranceprotection.com/death_vs_disability.

18 "The Complete 2023 Estate Planning Report." n.d. *LawDepot*. https://www.lawdepot.com/resources/estate-articles/ estate-planning-report/.

19 "The Future of Wealth in the United States Mapping Trends in Generational Wealth a Research Report from the Deloitte Center for Financial Services." n.d. https://www2.deloitte.com/content/ dam/insights/us/articles/us-generational-wealth-trends/ DUP_1371_Future-wealth-in-America_MASTER.pdf.

20 Internal Revenue Service. 2010. "Estate Tax | Internal Revenue Service." *irs.gov*. 2010. https://www.irs.gov/businesses/ small-businesses-self-employed/estate-tax.

21 "The Value of Financial Planning." n.d. https://www.fpcanada.ca/ docs/default-source/communications/ value-study.pdf.

www.ingramcontent.com/pod-product-compliance
Lightning Source LLC
Chambersburg PA
CBHW030509210326
41597CB00013B/849